Saint Pier Giorgio Frassati

SAINT PIER GIORGIO FRASSATI

An Ordinary Christian

By Maria Di Lorenzo

Translated by Robert Ventresca

Pauline
BOOKS & MEDIA
BOSTON

Library of Congress Control Number: 2025941681

ISBN 10: 0-8198-1926-3
ISBN 13: 978-0-8198-1926-0

Cover design by Daughters of St. Paul

Unless otherwise noted, photos courtesy of PAOLINE Editoriale Libri, Milan.

Originally published in Italy by PAOLINE Editoriale Libri, Milan.

First English edition, 2004.

Published by Pauline Books & Media, 50 Saint Paul's Avenue, Boston, MA 02130-3491.

Printed in the U.S.A.

www.pauline.org

Pauline Books & Media is the publishing house of the Daughters of St. Paul, an international congregation of women religious serving the Church with the communications media.

1 2 3 4 5 6 7 8 9 10 30 29 28 27 26 25

When I see my brothers,
I do not see brothers, but angels.
When I see a poor man entering my cell,
I bow my head before him,
recalling in my heart the words of Scripture:
"You have seen your brother,
you have seen your Lord."

— Paisj Velickovskij
Autobiography of a Staretz

Contents

Chronology

1901 Pier Giorgio Michelangelo Frassati, son of Alfredo and Adelaide Ametis Frassati, is born on April 6, at 6:00 P.M., and, because of lung problems, is baptized immediately.

1902 Pier Giorgio's sister, Luciana, is born on August 18.

1907 Pier Giorgio and Luciana begin their education at home.

1910 In June, Pier Giorgio makes his first confession.

The two Frassati children complete their elementary school exams at the Salesian Institute in July.

Pier Giorgio and Luciana enter Massimo D'Azeglio junior high school in October. One month later, the Salesian priest, Father Antonio Cojazzi, begins private lessons with the Frassati children.

1911 In June, Pier Giorgio receives his First Communion in the chapel of the Auxiliary Sisters of the Souls in Purgatory.

1913 Pier Giorgio fails Latin and enters the Jesuit-run Social Institute, where he attends his third year of junior high school.

1914 Pier Giorgio joins the Apostolate of Prayer and the Company of the Blessed Sacrament. In October, he and Luciana return to the D'Azeglio junior high school, where Pier Giorgio completes the fourth and fifth years.

1915 In June, Pier Giorgio receives the sacrament of Confirmation at Our Lady of Grace Church in Crocetta.

1917 Pier Giorgio receives a certificate in agricultural studies at Turin's Bonafous Institute.

Both Frassati children fail Latin. They return to the Social Institute in October.

1918 Pier Giorgio joins the Marian Sodality.

Pier Giorgio receives his high school diploma in October.

Pier Giorgio joins the Brotherhood of the Rosary in Pollone, the Saint Vincent Society at the Social Institute, and the Italian Alpine Club, remaining a member until his death. He begins courses in mechanical engineering at Turin's Royal Polytechnic, with the intention of specializing in mining engineering.

1920 Pier Giorgio joins the University Nocturnal Adoration group and the Young Workers group of

Santa Maria in Piazza. On December 4, he joins the Popular Party.

1921 Alfredo Frassati becomes ambassador to Germany, and Pier Giorgio goes with him to Berlin.

Pier Giorgio participates in the Tenth Congress of the Italian Federation of Catholic University Students.

Extended visit with the Rahner family in Freiberg, Germany.

1922 Pier Giorgio joins the Legion of Mary Club of Young Catholics in the parish Church of Crocetta.

In May, Pier Giorgio joins the Third Order Dominicans and takes the name Girolamo.

Pier Giorgio spends the months of November and December in Berlin.

1923 Following the French occupation of the Ruhr Valley, Germany, Pier Giorgio publishes a letter of support to German students on behalf of the Cesare Balbo University Club.

Pier Giorgio falls in love with Laura Hidalgo.

Pier Giorgio takes part in the opening of the meeting of the Italian Popular Party.

In May, Pier Giorgio is one of the first to join the Association of Friends of the Catholic University of the Sacred Heart.

Pier Giorgio resigns from the Cesare Balbo Club because their flag was displayed to honor Mussolini's visit to Turin.

1924 The Shady Characters Society is established.

Fascist hoodlums break into the Frassati house and Pier Giorgio manages to chase the intruders away.

1925 Pier Giorgio complains of a migraine and lack of appetite, which appear to be the symptoms of a normal case of the flu.

On July 1, Pier Giorgio's grandmother, Linda Copello Ametis, dies.

On July 4, at 7:00 P.M., Pier Giorgio Frassati dies of acute poliomyelitis.

A huge crowd gathers for Pier Giorgio's funeral on July 6.

1932 The Church officially opens the cause for Pier Giorgio's beatification (concluding on October 23, 1935).

1938 The Church issues the *nulla osta* decree, clearing the way for the beatification to move forward.

1941 Allegations from anonymous sources reach Rome and Pier Giorgio's cause is temporarily suspended.

1965 Pope Paul VI assigns the Jesuit Father Paolo Molinari with the task of conducting a further study of Frassati's life.

1978 Paul VI signs the introduction to the cause for beatification of the Servant of God Pier Giorgio Frassati.

1987 The *Positio super virtutibus* is presented, and on October 23 Pier Giorgio is declared Venerable.

1990 Pier Giorgio Frassati is beatified by Pope John Paul II on May 20.

Blessed Pier Giorgio's mortal remains are transferred to a side altar in the Cathedral of Turin.

2025 Pier Giorgio Frassati is canonized by Pope Leo XIV on September 7.

Preface

When my editor asked me to write this biography, I wondered with some perplexity if there was much point in writing a new book about Pier Giorgio Frassati. This young man from Turin, much beloved by people the world over, has had a great deal written about him in recent years. His charming and ever-contemporary image is constantly turning up in catecheses, at conferences, in sermons, in studies, and in journals—some 2,000 articles about Frassati have appeared in print in recent years. So why write more?

What I failed to realize, in my deliciously human logic, was the imponderable meaning of "chance," the sum total of seeming accidents Divine Providence enjoys scattering along life's path with a logic all God's own. And along my own path, both personal and professional, Pier Giorgio had been waiting for me from the start, so to speak; perhaps he has been waiting for some time.

Just as a person discovers a hidden figure in a game of connect-the-dots, so day after day I went in search of Pier Giorgio, tracing the footsteps of his life and character in order to sketch a spiritual biography that would tell of his joy, and somehow to explain the "unexplainable": his clear and extraordinary friendship with God.

In an address before the Seventeenth World Youth Day, held in Canada in July 2002, Pope John Paul II invited young people, whom he refers to as the "guardians of the morning," to consider the example of the saints:

> Just as salt gives flavor to food and light illumines the darkness, so too holiness gives full meaning to life and makes it reflect God's glory. How many saints, especially young saints, can we count in the Church's history! . . . Let us remember only a few of them: Agnes of Rome. . . . Thérèse of Lisieux, Pier Giorgio Frassati . . .
>
> Discover your Christian roots, learn about the Church's history, deepen your knowledge of the spiritual heritage which has been passed on to you, follow in the footsteps of the witnesses and teachers who have gone before you!

May young people the world over take the pope's words to heart and follow, as he urges, in the footsteps of these witnesses of faith, of that blessed and great crowd that has gone before us in love. Among them stands out the extraordinary figure of Pier Giorgio Frassati, an "ordinary" young man who truly lived the Beatitudes to the full during his brief lifetime. He is a modern-day saint, a young person just like young people today.

First, and foremost, I would like to thank my editor for giving me the opportunity to get to know such a splendid personality as Pier Giorgio Frassati, who was my companion for an entire year—the time it took me to complete this book.

I am certain that he will continue to accompany me in the future, in my journey as a believer, a woman, and a writer.

I would be grateful to readers who wish to share their impressions with me in writing via my contact page: https://mariaamata.it/contact-me, convinced that we benefit and nurture our unique faith in Christ, in the light of the communion of saints, through dialogue and an open, sincere sharing.

Introduction

Carmelite monasteries throughout the world have a tradition of circulating the biographies of their deceased Sisters. In the Carmel of Lisieux in 1897, Sister Thérèse of the Child Jesus died at the age of twenty-four. A Carmelite for only nine years, hers was a little-known, unremarkable, and seemingly insignificant life. What could her Sisters find to write in her biography? What could they say of her brief twenty-four years? Apparently nothing, at least from the perspective of the world at that time, but today we know better. Countless people the world over now venerate Saint Thérèse, declared a Doctor of the Church by Pope John Paul II, as one of the greatest saints in the history of the Church, and she foresaw this when before her death she said to the Sisters assisting her in the infirmary: "You are taking care of a little saint."[1]

Youth, so rich with promises that often disappoint and expectations that may never be realized, contains the seeds of sanctity. The young Carmelite nun, who died of tuberculosis while her life was so full of promise, lived her "little way" of simple and loving confidence in God, which has made her a much recognized and greatly admired teacher of the spiritual life.

The story of this young French woman has a great deal in common with the young Italian man, Pier Giorgio Frassati, who lived in Turin at the beginning of the twentieth century. His life on earth also passed swiftly, like a meteor setting the world on fire.

On March 13, 1983, only a few steps from Saint Peter's, John Paul II inaugurated the International Youth Center. The center is a place for young people from all over the world. It provides a warm welcome to young pilgrims, and offers them the opportunity to pray with the local Church and come to know the life of the diocese of Rome. During the inaugural ceremony, the Holy Father presented the center with a reproduction of the Cross of San Damiano, and turning to the young people present, he said:

> Together with the memory of the ancient cross of San Damiano, from the life of Saint Francis of Assisi, I also want to remind you of a young person who lived in our own time, Pier Giorgio Frassati, to encourage you to keep striving toward high ideals. . . .
>
> He lived all of the Beatitudes of the Gospel.

Indeed, Pier Giorgio was a typical young man: he studied, fell in love, enjoyed the company of his friends, and played practical jokes. He was involved in sports and politics. And he prayed. He grew up, as many young people do today, in an atmosphere strained by the difficult relationship between his parents, who lived "separated under one roof."

From black and white photographs of Pier Giorgio, one sees a young man with an honest, joyful face, his distinct features framed by thick black hair. His dark, deep eyes are alight with irresistible joy. Pier Giorgio Frassati is proof that holiness does not wear a sad face! People look more for actions than words, for lives that give flesh and blood to ideals, and Pier Giorgio Frassati's life and witness to his faith has inspired generations of young people. Even today, one hundred years after his birth, he continues, in the words of John Paul II, "to show us what it truly means for a young lay person to give a concrete answer to the call, 'Come, follow me.'"

Pier Giorgio could easily have become an idol for Turin's rich and famous, but he chose a life of sacrifice and love for "the least" members of society. He could have filled the hours of his youth with parties and dancing, but he preferred to be a "porter" for the poor, roaming the streets of Turin with his wheelbarrow full of household goods belonging to people evicted from their homes.

Although born into a wealthy and prominent family, Pier Giorgio did not want his father's money; he did not hide the fact that he intended to share the wealth he inherited from his father with the poor. As a university student, he undertook challenging studies for a degree in engineering in order to fulfill his dream of becoming a mining engineer, and dedicating himself to doing Christ's work among miners, who were the outcasts of the working class.

Dynamic, strong-willed, full of life, Pier Giorgio loved poetry, hikes in the mountains, flowers, music. He was an experienced skier and expert swimmer. He participated in many sports: sailing, canoeing, cycling, and horseback riding.

He was a sportsman who could move easily from bicycle to horse, from the beach to the mountains. The journalist Italo Alighiero Chiusano aptly described him as "an avalanche of life," always ready to have fun with his friends, kind and easily carried away, always in a hurry. Pier Giorgio took the Gospel seriously, and gave himself entirely to the things he believed in without being sanctimonious.

Pier Giorgio was all these things, and much more. The personal accounts and memories of those who knew him paint a portrait of an honest and strong young man, alive with joy, generous of heart, and full of faith. He was a rich young man who gave his unconditional, joyful "yes" to Christ's invitation: "follow me."

"What is the life of a saint," asked Saint Francis de Sales, "if not the Gospel put into practice?" And Pier Giorgio Frassati put the Gospel into practice by living it in his everyday circumstances. Though he could have lived an easy, stylish life, could have been a champion of worldliness, he felt the strong allure of Christ and followed it to the end.

Pier Giorgio Frassati's living out of the Gospel is extraordinary in its ordinariness. He lived the Gospel in every aspect of his life as naturally as one breathes, eats, and walks. His is a sanctity within the reach of every Christian. The author Stefano Jacomuzzi once wrote:

> I always liked Pier Giorgio. I liked him because in the search for examples he was a kind of counterbalance to the distant and puzzling images of great saints: martyrs, bishops, confessors, and hermits, those virtually unbelievable heroes armed with agony and worn out by fasting. If I absolutely had to pick a hero [Pier Giorgio] suits me best. . . . Yet, I do

not think of holiness . . . how can someone you meet on the street, someone just like you, a student with the same problems, including that hard-won breath of first love, how can such a person be a saint?

My idea of saintliness was mistaken. Better yet, I had only one idea of saintliness from reading and from sermons. . . . I did not think of grace, of the choice that transforms a positive response into heroic virtue. The rich young man of the Gospel could not bring himself to say "yes" to everything Christ asked. With simplicity, perhaps without even being aware of it himself, Pier Giorgio did just that: and so an abundance of attainable human virtues became heroism.[2]

Chapter 1

Idyllic Days

On Holy Saturday, April 6, 1901, in Turin, Italy, the first and only male child was born to Alfredo and Adelaide Frassati, one of the most well-known families of Turin. The couple's first child, Elda, had been born in 1899, but died eight months later. Alfredo Frassati wished to name his son after his own father, Pietro, who had died only two years before, but Adelaide disliked the name. They finally compromised and added the name Giorgio, after the warrior saint who had slain the dragon.

Pier Giorgio showed signs of asphyxia at birth and the family quickly summoned the parish priest, Father Alessandro Roccati, to come to baptize the infant at home. A few months later, on September 5, this "private" ceremony was followed with the pomp and circumstance of a public celebration at the parish church of Pollone.

Alfredo Frassati was born on September 28, 1868, in the town of Pollone in the Biellese province of the Piedmont region of Italy. He became the successful founder and director of the liberal newspaper, *La Stampa*. Adelaide Ametis, born in 1877 in Pallone, had a great passion for art. A student of some of Italy's most prominent artists, one of her portraits received critical acclaim while on display at Venice's Biennale Art Exhibit in 1912. Alfredo fell in love with Adelaide, who was his distant relative, and they were married on September 5, 1898.

At the age of twenty-two, Alfredo Frassati graduated from university with a degree in law, but his true interest lay in printed news media, which, in his opinion, represented a "new force" at the dawn of the twentieth century capable of guiding "all peoples to achieving the common good."

Alfredo demonstrated notable managerial skills in the publishing field and took over the newspaper, *Gazetta Piemontese*, reissuing it on January 1, 1895 under the new title: *La Stampa-Gazetta Piemontese*.

By 1907 *La Stampa* was publishing eight pages and reached the watermark of 100 thousand copies. From the end of the nineteenth century to 1915, the newspaper went from fifty thousand copies sold daily to some 300 thousand copies. In an effort to modernize production, Alfredo began using linotype, and enriched the paper with numerous supplements: *La Stampa sportiva* (1902), the first Italian sports journal; *La Donna* (1904), a bi-monthly supplement dedicated to women's issues; and *La Stampa agricola* (1912), dedicated to agricultural concerns. The Turin-based daily newspaper became one of the most respected in Italy.

Contributors to the newspaper included some of Italy's most prestigious figures of the time, including Guido Gozzano,

Associazione Pier Giorgio Frassati, Rome.

Alfredo Frassati and Adelaide Ametis in a photo before their marriage on September 5, 1898; both strong-willed and independent characters, theirs would be a strained and unhappy union.

Giuseppe Antonio Borgese, and the economist, Luigi Einaudi. Alfredo, a man of liberal ideas, was deeply loyal to the liberal politician, Giovanni Giolitti. Alfredo threw all of his energy into the paper, so much so that people thought of the two as one entity and it was often said: "*La Stampa* is Frassati!"[3]

With Alfredo's complete devotion to his work and Adelaide's complete absorption in her painting, it soon became evident that they had few common interests. Their marriage dragged on for years between arguments and misunderstandings, often bringing them to the verge of separation. Adelaide was a whimsical, hasty, and energetic character, and she could sometimes be spiteful. Alfredo, an authoritarian, recognized the many ways he and Adelaide were so much alike. The two clashed even before their marriage, and Alfredo had written to Adelaide, "We are far too similar to avoid these storms."

The delicate family situation, which was the source of much tension and pain, had a profound effect on Pier Giorgio's life, as well as that of his sister, Luciana, who was born at Pollone on August 18, 1902. Years later Luciana would recall the heavy atmosphere that hung over the Frassati home as "an ill-defined nightmare."

When Pier Giorgio began talking, he gave himself the nickname "Dodo." He began kindergarten in Pollone at the age of three, and it was there that he had his first contact with religious sentiments with lessons from the Compendium of Christian Doctrine, later known as the Catechism of Saint Pius X.

One day at school, Pier Giorgio was deeply troubled to learn that Saint Joseph was Jesus' foster father. He brooded over this at home for some time before finally asking his mother if that meant Jesus was an orphan. When Adelaide explained that, far from being an orphan, Jesus had two fathers, Pier Giorgio became happy once again.

Pier Giorgio was a lively, active child. At home, the Frassatis called him "Sonntagskind,"[4] a German nickname meaning "life of the party." Pier Giorgio loved noisy toys, racing, soccer, and bicycling. Luciana, always in tow, became his inseparable "partner in crime." When their maternal grandmother, Linda Copello Ametis, wanted to describe a heightened state of noise and confusion, she used two words: "Casa Frassati (the Frassati household)."

From his earliest years, Pier Giorgio demonstrated a strong and somewhat impulsive character. An exuberant and affectionate child, he always seemed to be in a good mood and, despite his young age, was very sensitive and compassionate toward others. Once, while he was in kindergarten, Pier Giorgio noticed an unhappy child sitting alone at lunchtime. The other children had shunned him because of his badly scarred face, the result of a terrible skin disease. Pier Giorgio immediately sat down beside the lonely boy and cheerfully shared his meal, even using the same spoon.

On another occasion, four-year-old Pier Giorgio heard someone knocking at the door at home and when he opened it, he saw a feeble woman holding a child in her arms. Pier Giorgio noticed the child's bare feet and he immediately took off his own shoes and socks and gave them to the woman. Then he quickly closed the door before anyone in the house realized what he had done.

Pier Giorgio prayed each night before going to bed. Dressed in his nightshirt, he would kneel on the mattress at the foot of his bed. With his rosary in hand little Pier Giorgio would pray—until he fell fast asleep, tumbling off the bed!

A sweet and mysterious Presence was already quietly speaking to his heart.

On June 11, 1910, Pier Giorgio and Luciana made their first confession at Turin's Corpus Domini Church. A year later, on June 19, 1911, they received their First Communion in the chapel of the Auxiliary Sisters of the Souls in Purgatory. The strictly private ceremony was followed by a simple reception consisting of a cup of hot chocolate. "They seemed like two newlyweds," was their mother's excited and somewhat frivolous comment that day. Adelaide was rather formal in matters of religion, which for her consisted of set practices and customs and duties to be performed at certain times, much like paying one's taxes. She taught her children prayers that they were to say on their knees in the morning and at night; she never missed Sunday Mass, but Pier Giorgio would later say that he had never seen her receive Communion.

For his part, though he was an agnostic, Alfredo agreed to allow his children to receive religious instruction. A sensible and progressive man, he placed all his faith in the secular values disseminated in his newspaper. Even as a child, Pier Giorgio could not have differed more from his father. One afternoon, in 1908, the seven-year-old Pier Giorgio ran up to his mother in tears. "Mama," he cried, "there was a poor, hungry man at the door and Papa did not give him anything to eat!" Alfredo had encountered a man begging for charity at the entrance of the house, but seeing that he was drunk, Alfredo sent him away immediately. Pier Giorgio witnessed this and was terribly disturbed because he was convinced that Jesus had come to the house and that his father had sent him away hungry.

Adelaide tried to calm Pier Giorgio, but she could not. Only when she sent someone to fetch the beggar back to the house in order to give him something to eat and drink was Pier Giorgio satisfied. Later, Adelaide found that the man had indeed been lying about his neediness, and she said as much to her son. This did not deter Pier Giorgio, however, and he persisted: "But what if it was Jesus who sent us that poor man?"

Luciana recalls that "his personal relationship with God helped Pier Giorgio to mature more quickly, and ended with his gradual detachment from the rest of the family."[5] In fact, given the situation at the Frassati home, when it came to matters of faith Pier Giorgio was always self-educated. Pier Giorgio loved to pray, curled up with his small prayer book in hand, to mediate in silence, and to sit in adoration of the Blessed Sacrament where he found his very best friend and the Teacher who spoke to his heart. No one taught this to Pier Giorgio; he learned it from God, as we read in the prophet Jeremiah: "I will put my law within them, and I will write it on their hearts" (31:33).

The Frassati children spent all their time together. In fact, their parents did not allow them to play with other children, not even as they became older. They were raised in an atmosphere of prohibitions and sacrifices—early to bed at night, a

Associazione Pier Giorgio Frassati, Rome.

Pier Giorgio, shown here at the age of four when he gave away his shoes and socks to a poor woman whose child was barefoot.

Pier Giorgio and his sister, Luciana, were only a year apart in age. Luciana would be Pier Giorgio's closest friend and confidante.

The Frassati family at the villa in Pollone during their summer vacation of 1910. The villa was Pier Giorgio's treasured refuge from the city.

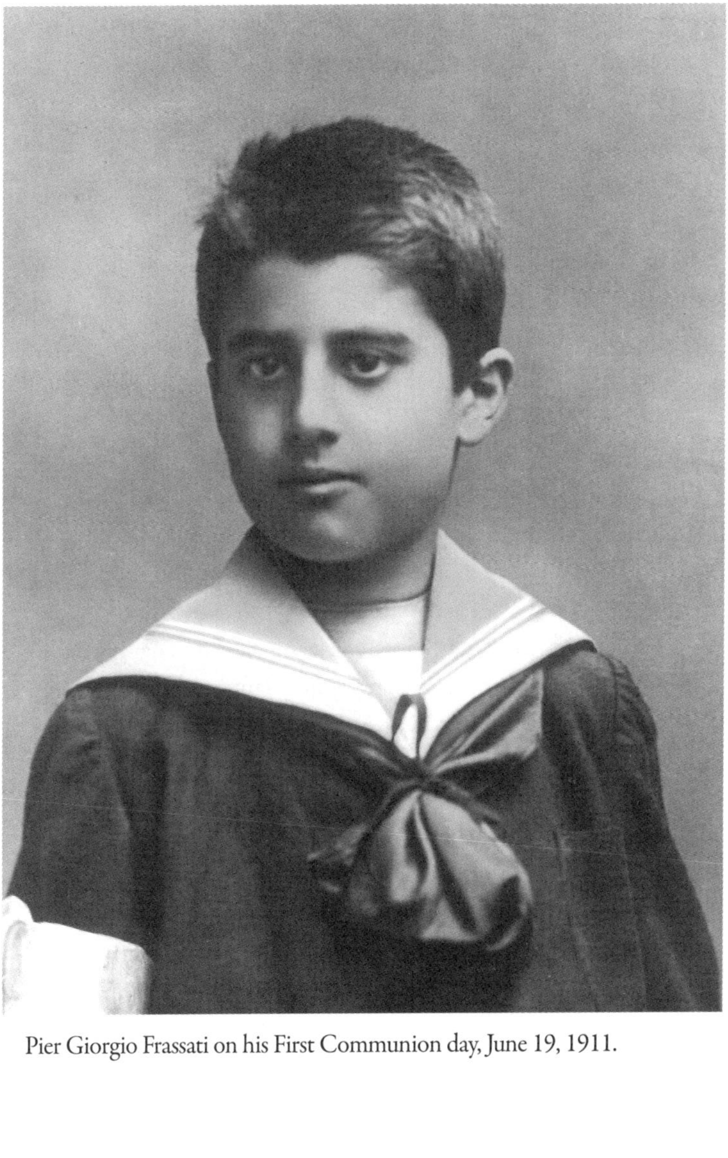

Associazione Pier Giorgio Frassati, Rome.

Pier Giorgio Frassati on his First Communion day, June 19, 1911.

splash of cold water early in the morning whether winter or summer—they were even forbidden to walk the streets of the city by themselves, or to linger in front of newsstands or store windows. Discipline and obedience was the principal rule in everything. Dialogue between parents and a child at that time was virtually nonexistent, and so honor, respect, and fear governed their relationship.

In the autumn of 1907, Pier Giorgio and Luciana began their schooling at home with Rosina Buratto as their tutor. The arrangement lasted until 1910 when the Frassati children entered the Salesian Institute in Alassio to complete their elementary school studies.

When he learned to write, Pier Giorgio felt duty-bound to pen brief letters to his parents and relatives for various occasions. Pier Giorgio wrote his first letter when he was about six years old:

> My dearest little daddy. I love you so much and to make you happy, I won't hit Luciana anymore. Happy holiday. I will pray to Baby Jesus for you. Kisses, your Dodo.[6]

Actually, Pier Giorgio did not care much for writing—a nightmare to him because of his dislike for grammar and punctuation. He preferred to spend time playing and in the mountains.

The Frassati home was a common gathering place of well-known authors, journalists, and other important personalities including Guido Gozzano, Giuseppe Antonio Borgese, and Salvatore Gotta, but Pier Giorgio had little interest in such company. Alfredo Frassati had high expectations for his only son, but he soon found himself disappointed in the boy. Pier

Giorgio lacked his father's ambition and seriousness. He was rarely "at his books," preferring to have fun with his friends. He was becoming a very different son from the one Alfredo dreamed of, and Pier Giorgio was growing apart from the world into which he was born.

At the beginning of each summer, the Frassatis left for some vacation time in Pollone, their charming hometown with its narrow, winding streets lined with antique houses and high walls and gates that protected quaint villas bathed in flowering gardens. One of these villas belonged to Adelaide's father, Francesco Ametis. A pharmacist, who had volunteered to fight in the Crimean War, Francesco had later immigrated to Peru and made a modest fortune. When Francesco returned to Italy, he built the villa in Pollone, and planted a giant South American sequoia tree in its lovely garden.

The time the Frassatis spent at their villa at Pollone, in the an atmosphere enriched with luxuriant greenery and flowers, was a treasured haven. "Peaceful Pollone," as Pier Giorgio referred to the villa, was always a happy place for him, a place where he could dream, restore his spirit, escape the stress of city life, and be in touch with the nature he had grown to love.

The family had a small "zoo" at the villa with pet dogs, cats, birds, and a goat, and the Frassatis raised sheep, horses, poultry, and other barnyard animals. Pier Giorgio loved animals and he had special affection for Mime, Wotan, and Uadi—the dogs and cats he named after characters from operas by the German composer Richard Wagner.

From his bedroom, Pier Giorgio could see the Mucrone River, which dominates the entire town of Pollone. When the weather was good, Pier Giorgio would go down into the garden, climb a tree, and balance himself on one of the larger branches. He made this his desk, reviewing his homework aloud and reciting favorite lines from Dante and the Psalms from the tree. Pier Giorgio would also sing, quite out of tune, at the top of his lungs so that neighbors and passersby could hear him.

The days spent at Pollone were idyllic. Pier Giorgio enjoyed playing, digging in the garden, and carting wood, baskets of fruit, and fertilizer to help the gardener. Each evening he insisted on giving the gardener a hand in watering the grounds—a difficult task that meant carrying 120 cans of water—so that the work was shared equally.

In October 1910, the Frassati children, both dressed in "sailor suits," began classes at the Massimo D'Azeglio, one of Turin's most prestigious public middle schools. Some time later, Father Antonio Cojazzi began tutoring the Frassati children. The Salesian priest, originally from Friuli in the province of Udine, was an excellent teacher and a jovial man. Father Cojazzi, Saint Pier Giorgio's first biographer, remembered how "hurrying to complete his homework, Pier Giorgio would get up from his seat, plant himself in front of me with his arms folded, and, looking at me with his big, dark eyes, would ask, 'And now will you tell me a story about Jesus?'"[7]

The Gospel was a magnet pulling on Pier Giorgio's heart and predisposing him toward works of charity. Luciana recalled, "He was barely eleven years old, but already his mind was occupied with the thought of others' sufferings, which he tried to alleviate with small gestures, like collecting foil paper, tram tickets, and stamps for missionaries."[8] Often Pier Giorgio's uncle Pietro gave him money, which always promptly went into the pockets of the poor. The same thing happened with the money he asked of his paternal grandmother Giuseppina. The ten or twenty lire she suggested Pier Giorgio deposit in the bank he would quickly invest in another "bank" that returned one hundred to one.

Chapter 2

Joys and Sorrows

As Pier Giorgio completed his second year at the Massimo D'Azeglio in October 1913, he failed Latin. He hastened to write his strict father about this failure:

> Dear Papa,
>
> I am confused and miserable; I saw how much this hurt Mama, and I thought of how much it will hurt you, so much so that I don't know how to beg your forgiveness. . . . I only hope that you will continue to believe me when I say how hard I plan to study this year. . . . You will see that I will show my love in deeds.[9]

Forced to abandon public school, Pier Giorgio began his third year of middle school at the Social Institute run by the Jesuits. It was here that Pier Giorgio met the Jesuit priest Father Lombardi, the man responsible for the spiritual formation of the students. Never had failing a course proved so providential.

An active and exuberant boy, Pier Giorgio *(second from the left)* skates with his sister Luciana *(far left)* and their mother, Adelaide *(to Pier Giorgio's right)*, in this photo taken in 1911.

Associazione Pier Giorgio Frassati, Rome.

Twelve-year-old Pier Giorgio with his father in a photo taken in 1913, the year Alfredo was elected to the Senate in Italy.

Father Lombardi introduced Pier Giorgio to the beauty of the daily reception of Jesus in the Holy Eucharist, and Pier Giorgio became immediately enthused. However, still a minor, he had to have his mother's consent, and Adelaide did not agree at all. She worried that daily reception of the Eucharist would make it a mere habit emptied of meaning. Perhaps she also worried that her son might feel an attraction to the priestly vocation. Adelaide, who already considered her son too "sanctimonious," certainly felt concern that her only son could become a priest. As set as Adelaide was against Pier Giorgio's request, Pier Giorgio also refused to yield. After several days of the wrestling of wills, Pier Giorgio managed to convince his mother. One morning Pier Giorgio entered Father Lombardi's office exclaiming, "Father, I have won!" Father Lombardi, acting as if he had not guessed the reason for Pier Giorgio's happiness, asked what he could possibly have won to make him so happy, jokingly suggesting the lottery. "Much more than that, Father," Pier Giorgio responded. "I can now receive Jesus every morning!"

From that day until the very last of his life, Pier Giorgio always received Communion. Thus, the Eucharist became the focus of his day: He fasted from midnight and got up early every morning to keep his "appointment" with the Lord. It was not unusual for him to forgo an excursion with friends rather than miss receiving Communion.

In October 1914, Pier Giorgio returned to the Massimo D'Azeglio to complete his fourth and fifth years. Cheerful, boisterous, and always ready to create a stir, Pier Giorgio was like any other student in his class. His classmates called him "Fracassati," a play on his surname and the Italian *fracasso*,

Enamored of nature, the twelve-year-old Pier Giorgio hiking in the mountains (1913).

meaning "racket" or "noise." Pier Giorgio had such a bad habit of turning around to make a face, chat, or laugh with his friends sitting behind him that his teacher, Giovanni Masera, good-naturedly nicknamed him "Giano Bifronte," after the two faced Roman god, Janus.

On June 28, 1914, a Serbian nationalist assassinated Archduke Francis Ferdinand of Austria and his wife Sofia at Sarajevo, capital of Bosnia and Herzegovina. Soon all of Europe was engulfed in the flames of war.

In Italy, people were intensely divided in a debate over the conflict. There were those who favored involvement in the war and those who favored neutrality. Student marches spilled into public squares, while Gabriele D'Annunzio[10] issued declarations in favor of joining the war, which most people expected to be short with certain victory for the Allied Powers. Italian Prime Minister Giolitti disagreed, and Alfredo Frassati's *La Stampa* supported Giolitti's position.

The disputes that broke out at the D'Azeglio often ended in a scuffle. Only three of the D'Azeglio's students were in favor of Italian neutrality: Pier Giorgio and Luciana Frassati, and Camillo Banzatti, the son of the vice-president of *La Stampa*.

The fourteen-year-old Pier Giorgio felt great disappointment when, on May 24, 1915, Italy declared war on Austria, an event that led to one of the few times in Pier Giorgio's life when he fought. One day, as Pier Giorgio and Camillo Banzatti were walking down a street of Turin, Mario Attilio

Levi (the future historian) began jeering at them, "You are traitors, just like your fathers. Mercenaries!" The accusation suggested that Frassati and Banzatti had sold out Italy to the Central Powers. Camillo grabbed Mario by the neck and let him have it while Pier Giorgio stood by and did nothing. When his parents heard about the incident, they told Pier Giorgio that he had been a coward for failing to defend himself. Pier Giorgio calmly answered, "It was two against one; tomorrow, it's my turn." In fact, the next day Pier Giorgio met up with Mario Attilio Levi and said to him, "Yesterday, it was Camillo who gave it to you, today it's my turn."

Pier Giorgio felt profound sadness at the harsh reality of the First World War, which claimed countless numbers of innocent lives. For all the rhetoric and excitement of interventionists, the war revealed its true face not in military displays and fanfare, but in a great slaughter, a "useless massacre" as Pope Benedict XV said in his strong condemnation of the war.

Deeply troubled, Pier Giorgio spent more time in prayer, asking the Lord for an end to the conflict. Among the Frassati's servants was a young woman, Natalina, whose brother had already died in battle. One day Pier Giorgio asked Natalina, "Wouldn't you give your own life to stop the war?" "Of course not!" the woman responded quickly. Pier Giorgio looked at her intently and said, "I would give my own life, I would this very day."

When Pier Giorgio learned of the signing of the armistice in November 1918, he was so filled with joy at the news of peace that he rang the bells of the town of Pollone at length.

On June 10, 1915, at the parish church of Our Lady of Grace in Crocetta, Pier Giorgio and Luciana received the sacrament of Confirmation from Bishop Castrale, auxiliary bishop of Turin. In October, Pier Giorgio made his first trip to Rome, the cradle of Christianity, and immediately fell in love with the Eternal City.

When Pier Giorgio was fifteen years old, he and his friend, Camillo Banzatti, smoked their first cigars, and it became a habit for Pier Giorgio. Strange as it may seem for that day and age, Pier Giorgio's mother regularly smoked a pipe and cigars. When anyone tried to advise him against this bad habit, Pier Giorgio would respond jokingly, "What do you expect? My mother smoked a pipe when she was breast-feeding me!"

Pier Giorgio was always ready to play a joke or have a "friendly fight," as Luciana described his irresistible ways. Pier Giorgio Frassati was a seeming volcano of happiness and daring. His motto, "To serve the Lord in total happiness," was the force behind all his actions. Pier Giorgio's joyful living of his Christian vocation stood in sharp contrast to the words in George Bernanos' *I grandi cimiteri sotto la luna*: "Where in the devil's name do you [Christians] hide your happiness?" Admittedly, too often Christianity is not joyful, even if the Gospel, in name and content, is an announcement of joy, of "good news." Pier Giorgio believed and lived that good news. As one of his admirers said, "The happiness that radiated from his face could only come from an awareness of his friendship with God."[11]

Pier Giorgio possessed an extraordinary zest for life and he was everyone's friend. His self-giving was sometimes the cause of embarrassment, since he cared more about the poor than about his own appearance or the elegance proper for his social class. He certainly was not the "little gentleman from a good family" that everyone expected. "You ask me if I am happy," Pier Giorgio once wrote to Luciana. "How can I not be happy? So long as my faith gives me strength, I will always be happy!"[12]

As a student, Pier Giorgio did not regularly apply himself to his studies, but the few classes he failed were merely road-blocks along the way and never a measure of his intelligence or abilities. His scholastic "mishaps," if one may call them that, masked his thirst for knowledge and his passion for the literary works of great writers such as Shakespeare, Virgil, Dante, Manzoni, and Foscolo. He also had a hunger for the writings of the German author Johann Wolfgang von Goethe, the Letters of Saint Paul, the works of Saint Augustine, Girolamo Savonarola, and Saint Catherine of Siena. Pier Giorgio also cultivated diverse interests: music, art, drama, and photography.

On June 15, 1917, Pier Giorgio was awarded a certificate in agriculture by the Bonafous Institute of Turin. He had taken courses in this particular subject in order to be of some help to the wife of the Frassatis' gardener, who was fighting in the war. The final exam for the certificate required Pier Giorgio to harvest, bundle, and store hay, a task he managed remarkably well. He loved the idea of working the land.

Pier Giorgio was never a brilliant student, though he did well in history, geography, and math. He had a good memory, but his performance left much to be desired, as in the case of a course in Latin that both he and Luciana failed in the autumn of 1917. This failure prompted Alfredo and Adelaide to remove their children from public school and send them to the Jesuit-run Social Institute in Turin.

The Jesuits had established the Social Institute in 1881 as a school for the children of the higher social classes. The goal of the institute was to teach Christian values to future generations of leaders. Ultimately, the Jesuits sought to combat the decades-long prevalence of liberal, anticlerical, and Masonic influence.

While at the Institute, Pier Giorgio became intensely involved in various religious and social organizations. He joined the Eucharistic Crusade, the Association of the Most Blessed Sacrament, the Eucharistic League, and the Apostolate of Prayer, a thriving group begun in France in 1844 under the guidance of the Jesuit priest Father Francesco Saverio Gautrelet.

His experience with the Jesuit fathers refined Pier Giorgio's religious sensibility, leading him toward deeper prayer and devotion to the Blessed Sacrament, as well as a growing spirit of service and of love of neighbor, in whom he saw the very image of God. One day when he and his friends were entering the Institute with their usual racket, Pier Giorgio noticed that the school custodian, a man named Fassone, looked terribly sad. Pier Giorgio broke away from his friends and approached Fassone to ask if something was wrong. With a quivering voice, Fassone broke down saying, "Yesterday, I buried my son . . . he was only fourteen years old!" Pier Giorgio stayed to comfort the grieving father. On the first anniversary of the death of Fassone's son, Pier Giorgio sought out the custodian to say, "I prayed for your son at Communion this morning."

Chapter 3

A Stranger in Turin

In October of 1918, Pier Giorgio received his high school diploma, completing in one year the requirements for the second and third year. One month later, he enrolled in the mechanical engineering program at the Royal Polytechnic of Turin. He intended to specialize in mining engineering to fulfill his dream of working beside miners and helping to improve the working and living conditions of that highly exploited group.

The curriculum at the Polytechnic was demanding and Pier Gïorgio took his studies seriously. His academic progress was never noteworthy, but it was consistent. Pier Giorgio had a more practical, concrete type of intelligence and he found it difficult to study for his exams. In fact, he sometimes had to put off taking a final exam because he was not adequately prepared.

In 1923, the Polytechnic became the official Royal School of Engineering. For the students, this change meant a more rigorous program of studies, which provoked a lively protest on the part of many students, including Pier Giorgio. The faculty was distinguished, but also very demanding, and if one wished to graduate, one had to work hard day and night. Pier Giorgio studied as hard as possible. Throughout his university years, he would spend entire days with his nose in the books, taking breaks only for prayer. For Pier Giorgio, prayer was as essential as the air he breathed and his work on behalf of the poor.

The city of Turin was teeming with poor people in the early 1900s. The influx of some fifty thousand people had transformed the old capital of the Savoyard dynasty into a major industrial center. The immigrants were mostly laborers who had left their homes in other regions of Italy in search of a better life in the so-called "industrial triangle" of Turin, Genoa, and Milan. These immigrants were often illiterate people who received meager pay for their hard work and lived in overcrowded lodgings in the concrete jungles on the outskirts of the city. Theirs was a miserable, sometimes inhumane existence.

These immigrants to the city were among the poorest of the poor, and their survival depended largely on the charitable works of individuals and organizations. One organization that devoted much of its resources to immigrant workers was the Saint Vincent de Paul Society, founded in Paris by Federic Ozanam several years earlier with the help of seven of his friends.

Pier Giorgio Frassati had joined the Social Institute's branch of the Saint Vincent de Paul Society on November 29, 1918. As a member of the society, Pier Giorgio visited families in need of moral support and material assistance. Pier Giorgio usually made these visits early in the morning, before his classes began at the university, or later in the evening. Whatever time of day, he always went with his arms full of packages to distribute, relying on the force of love to overcome the nauseating atmosphere in some of the hovels he visited.

Pier Giorgio also gave away his own money, often not leaving himself enough to pay for a train ride home. When he returned home late for the family's dinner, out of breath after running home, his annoyed mother would reprimand him, saying, "You are fundamentally good for nothing, so you could at least arrive on time!"[13] Pier Giorgio never defended or excused himself, but took his seat at the dinner table in silence, patiently bearing his family's misunderstanding. As Luciana would say many years later, "who could have understood the grandeur of his secret life?"[14]

No one at home knew of Pier Giorgio's visits to the poor. The Frassatis worried about what would become of their "strange" son who always had his head in the clouds and was so unlike his parents. "You will grow to become a useless man, to others and to yourself," his father once stated in frustration and concern. At the same time, Alfredo was remarkably in awe of his son, and never refused Pier Giorgio anything he asked, to the extent that he allowed Pier Giorgio to take the money from his pockets to bring to the poor. Alfredo even agreed to publish in *La Stampa* the many letters Pier Giorgio wrote on behalf of the poor. Years later, Alfredo recalled of his relationship with Pier Giorgio, "I never once accepted orders from anyone, not even from Giolitti. One person and one person alone had authority over me, and that was my son."[15] Ultimately, Pier Giorgio became the kind of person Alfredo wanted to be himself, and could have been if only he had had faith.

On November 13, 1913, at the age of forty-five, the wealthy owner of *La Stampa* was named to the Italian senate. Alfredo Frassati was the youngest senator in Italy—and the first journalist—with Prime Minister Giolitti's blessing. In 1920, the Italian government named Alfredo Italy's Ambassador to Germany. The Frassati family eventually joined him in Berlin, spending time between living there and in Pollone and Turin.

Pier Giorgio arrived in Berlin on March 3, 1921, and he wrote his grandmother, Josephine Frassati, "I hope to familiarize myself quickly with the Catholic student and workers' movements here so that I can keep up the same practices I had in Turin."[16] The fancy-free social atmosphere Luciana enjoyed so much at the Italian Embassy did not interest Pier Giorgio at all. Instead, he went in search of the poor and needy of Berlin. Many people had been reduced to poverty by the devaluation of German currency, and they lived day to day amid tremendous moral and material suffering. Germany was paying the price of an inflation caused by the cost of colossal war reparations imposed by the Treaty of Versailles.[17] There was widespread poverty in Berlin, and the haughty attitude of the French officials, strolling along the city's streets, only accentuated the poverty of ordinary Germans and made the situation more disheartening.

Pier Giorgio began to move about in the circles of German Catholic students and workers. He met Father Karl Sonneschein, a prominent figure of Catholic social action in Germany. Born in Düsseldorf in 1876, Sonneschein, a priest and a sociologist, was the chief organizer of the German Catholic Movement, and maintained a close relationship with the Italian Catholic Worker's Movement. In fact, after studying theology in Bonn and Rome, Sonneschein helped a group of Italian Catholics to establish the Popular Union in 1906. Back in Germany, he worked to promote the establishment of Catholic students' clubs in all the universities, giving life to groups made up of both workers and students. In 1918, Sonneschein established the General Office of Labor, the Catholic People's University, the Catholic Artists' Club, and he even became editor of Berlin's Catholic newspaper.

Sonneschein, nicknamed "the Saint Francis of Berlin," lived a life of utter poverty until the day he died in 1929. Pier Giorgio was profoundly influenced by this truly fascinating man. When he returned to Italy, Pier Giorgio translated what he had learned in Germany into a call for collaboration across the barriers among Catholic intellectuals and workers.

Pier Giorgio stayed in Berlin until June 5, 1921. In the autumn of that year, he went to Freiberg and stayed at the home of the Rahners. Of their seven children, Hugo and Karl would soon join the Jesuit Order. Pier Giorgio enjoyed his time in Freiberg, taking in the sites, especially the museums and art galleries of the city where he admired the works of Monet, Rubens, Segantini, and Rembrandt.

Louise Rahner, mother of the future theologian, Karl, later recalled:

> One morning, I was going to church with Pier Giorgio and I asked him what he wanted to do when he finished school. He told me that he had thought of becoming a priest, but then added, "I want to do whatever I can to help my people, and I think I can do this better as a layman than as a priest, because at home priests are not in such close contact with the people as they are here in Germany. By giving good example as a mining engineer, I can actually be much more effective."

Pier Giorgio's personal experience of the effectiveness of Sonneschein's work contrasted with that of the Italian clergy, often either too indolent or rendered virtually powerless by socio-political obstacles. Pier Giorgio believed he had to remain free to be able to do his good works, and so he determined to remain a layperson, though a part of him felt strongly attracted to the priestly vocation. In any event, it is unlikely that Alfredo and Adelaide would have permitted their only son to become a priest had he chosen this path. Once, when a nun asked Adelaide what she thought of the idea of Pier Giorgio becoming a priest, she answered abruptly, "I would rather he graduate from the university and die."[18]

Pier Giorgio demonstrated equal fervor in carrying out charitable works in Berlin as he had in Turin. He continued to neglect his own needs in order to help the poor. As he wrote to a classmate who would soon enter a convent, "It was there [in Germany] that I learned that one could live quite well indeed on just one meal a day." His father was an ambassador, but the lifestyle of the rich and famous never appealed to Pier Giorgio. Often, he took flowers from the vases in the embassy's offices and placed them on the coffins of the poor. Pier Giorgio declined invitations to attend the social events of fashionable society so that he would be free to go wherever the poor needed him. Once, in the dead of winter, he returned to the Italian Embassy without his coat, having given it away to some poor beggar he had met on the street. Pier Giorgio was simply following the example of Jesus, who said to his disciples:

> If any want to become my followers, let them deny themselves and take up their cross and follow me. For those who want to save their life will lose it, and those who lose their life for my sake will find it. For what will it profit them if they gain the whole world but forfeit their life? (Mt 16:24–26)

In 1922 Pier Giorgio wrote to his friend, Gian Maria Bertini, "With every day that passes, I fall more and more in love with the Germans."[19] Germany had become his home away from home, and he had forged many close friendships there. It is no surprise, then, that Pier Giorgio was deeply saddened when he had to return to Italy. In a note to his friend, Willibald Leitgebel, Pier Giorgio wrote, "I wanted to do so much for the Germans, but, unfortunately, there is nothing I can do. Please take this money for the poor children of Berlin. It isn't much, but I guess it is better than nothing."[20]

On January 11, 1923, in response to Germany's failure to pay the reparations stipulated by the Treaty of Versailles, France began its occupation of the Ruhr Valley. The German government responded by organizing a "passive resistance" that took the form of a general strike on January 22. The occupation also provoked violent clashes, which culminated on March 31 with the death of thirteen German workers.

As Pier Giorgio watched a bastion of German Catholic social democracy fall, he described the French occupation of the Ruhr Valley as a "disgrace"[21] in a letter to his friend, Antonio Villani.

Pier Giorgio wrote a letter of support to all German students on behalf of the Cesare Balbo University Club, a courageous gesture that had some impact. The letter, dated January 12, 1923, was published in the Deutsche Reichs Zeitung:

> In these tragic and painful moments in which your country is trampled upon by foreign feet, while your enemy occupies your home and hearth, we Catholic students extend to you an expression of our brotherly love.
>
> We are not able to change the sad situation, but we feel within us all the strength of our Christian love that binds us as brothers across national boundaries. Govern-ments today ignore the warning of the Holy Father: "True Peace is more a fruit of Christian love of neighbor than of justice," and instead they prepare humanity for future wars.
>
> Modern society is sinking into the sufferings caused by human passions and is moving away from every ideal of

love and of peace. As Catholics, we must bring that breath of goodness which can only come from faith in Christ.

Brothers, in your hour of darkness, know that the entire Christian family prays for you. . . . Since peace in the world can never come about without God, it is up to you, men of good faith, to keep in your hearts he who in the manger was declared by the angels to be the Savior of the World.

Pier Giorgio kept secret from his family his desire to work in Germany after graduating with a degree in mining engineering. As he wrote to Antonio Villani, "In a few years, God willing, I will be working in the Ruhr, and, as a Catholic, I will do what I can to help the Germans in their recovery."[22] The idea of being in Italy again did not please Pier Giorgio in the least. "Here I am again, in this troubled country. You know, I left Germany with much regret, because I greatly admire the character of the German people. Here in Italy, people change their minds like the wind, and on top of that there is no real freedom; I feel more like a foreigner in Turin than in Germany."[23] The pessimism Pier Giorgio expressed had a specific reason: Fascism.[24]

On October 28, 1922, Benito Mussolini[25] and the Fascists seized power in the infamous "March on Rome." The same day, an obviously upset Pier Giorgio wrote to his sister:

Dear Luciana,

Tomorrow I am leaving Turin for Pollone, and this time I do so quite eagerly. . . . I didn't get much schoolwork

> done today, but it is really not my fault; how can we remain calm at a tragic time like this. All kinds of ideas were racing through my head so that I couldn't concentrate on the physics of construction . . . I will leave it there for now, otherwise my pen will lead me to say something rude.[26]

A month later, Pier Giorgio was once again in Germany when he read Mussolini's famous speech to the Italian Parliament. Mussolini's words made Pier Giorgio's blood boil.

Again, writing to Villani from Berlin, Pier Giorgio admitted:

> I cannot wait to graduate so that I can remain in this beautiful country [Germany] where people still have a sense of their own responsibility and a conscience. Though it is sad to say, we have to admit that the Christian poet Dante was right when he said, "Ah servile Italy, hostel of grief, / ship without a pilot, in a great tempest, / no mistress of provinces, but brothel."[27] I am off now to find my friends so that we can discuss our business. You would not believe how happy I am to be here in a place so calm and so far removed from our poor country that has fallen into the hands of a bunch of scoundrels.[28]

Immediately after Mussolini seized power, Alfredo Frassati resigned his position as ambassador to Berlin. At the time he said, "I must resign right away, or my Giorgetto will not understand his father's conduct," words that certainly reflect Alfredo's awareness of Pier Giorgio's feelings toward the new Fascist government. Pier Giorgio recognized the true face of Fascism from the first, and he would call it "a party without ideas or ideals." A staunch opponent, Pier Giorgio often paid a personal price for his beliefs.[29] People at the university knew his views, and more than once Pier Giorgio came home from school bruised and with his clothes in shreds.[30]

Italy was caught in a tragic spiral of violence and hatred. On June 10, 1924, Fascist thugs murdered the Socialist parliamentarian, Giacomo Matteoti, for the "crime" of criticizing the Fascist's illegal tactics in parliament. Only a year earlier, on August 23, 1923, Fascist thugs from Ferrara brutally murdered Father Giovanni Minzoni, parish priest from Argenta. It was a grave moment in Italian history, as the country quickly marched toward a Fascist dictatorship. The atmosphere was charged with an approaching storm.

Chapter 4

Serving God in Others

In 1871, the Holy See issued a Non expedi[31] forbidding Catholics from voting in elections, reasoning that politics was the affair of "others," and good Christians should not be involved in an area of life that had nothing to do with matters of faith.

The 1871 decree endured several decades until Pope Benedict XV formally revoked it in 1919. However, in 1913, the "Gentiloni Agreement" at least finally opened the door for Christians to participate in public life. Gentiloni was then President of the Catholic Electoral Union, and he made it his mission to lead Italian Catholics into the political life of the country. In the elections of 1913, 208 Catholic deputies were elected to parliament. Spurred on by this success, and in keeping with the social teachings of Pope Leo XIII's encyclical, *Rerum Novarum* (1891), Father Luigi Sturzo established the Italian Popular Party, later simply referred to as the "Catholic Party."[32]

Politically active even as a student of the Polytechnic University of Turin, Pier Giorgio wore the badge of the Catholic Party despite the personal risks involved.

Responding to Father Sturzo's call for all "the free and the strong" to join the new party, Pier Giorgio signed up on December 4, 1920. In Turin, the party was a minor political force sandwiched between the liberal middle classes and the active working class movement organized by the Socialist party. In the 1919 national elections, Turin elected 100 Catholic deputies and the Socialists 156 as representatives to Rome.[33]

Pier Giorgio deeply admired Father Sturzo, and he was actively involved in the 1921 election campaign. Given the difficult political situation, the Catholic Party opted to present itself in a coalition with the Liberals. Pier Giorgio would have preferred that the Catholic Party present itself as independent, but this did not stop him from throwing himself wholeheartedly into the campaign, engaging in debates, putting up posters, campaigning in factories and even in the offices of the opposing parties. Despite the widespread pessimism that most people felt on the eve of that important election, Pier Giorgio was confident of victory.

The Catholic Party did become part of Mussolini's first coalition government in November 1922, but Pier Giorgio was disappointed with their role. "Where are our beautiful policies now? Where is the faith that animates our members?" he asked. "Unfortunately, when it comes to climbing the ladder of worldly success, men tend to trample on their own conscience."[34]

In April 1923, Pier Giorgio helped to organize the Annual Meeting of the Italian Popular Party in Turin. Father Sturzo wanted to extract the Catholic Party from its thorny collaboration with Mussolini. But, in order to avoid splitting the party and endangering its survival, Sturzo agreed to a compromise: the Catholic Party passed a motion pledging to support the government in parliament, but leaving itself the option of openly criticizing its policies.

In late January 1923, Pier Giorgio lamented in a letter to his German friend, Willibald Leitgebel: "We have lost the greatest gift God has given all of us, that is, freedom, without which life would be unbearable."[35] Sadly, the gradual rise of Mussolini's Fascist dictatorship was made possible in part by the support he received from some moderate members of the Popular Party. Pier Giorgio compared these moderates to the changing signals at a railway crossing. He wrote to Antonio Villani:

> What do you think of these switch signals who sell out to Fascism on a daily basis, as the paper *Il Momento* has just done? It sickens me more each day, and if I were not certain that my faith is of divine origin, I would likely do something crazy. But the one thing that keeps me from such thoughts is the assurance of a better life to come, if we work to do good here on earth. So let us get to work, and let us be sure to stick together to support each other and to spur each other forward on the path of goodness.[36]

Pier Giorgio was dismayed by the decision of the owners of *Il Momento* to support Mussolini's government because he had supported the paper and, to his father's chagrin, had even helped to publicize it. An irritated Alfredo Frassati once quipped sarcastically, "Good job, Pier Giorgio. I hear that you are a publicist for *Il Momento*. I assume, then, that when you are hungry, you will go to *Il Momento* for supper?"[37]

As the son of a founding father of modern Italian journalism, Pier Giorgio understood almost instinctively how important the press was in the struggle between different ideas. In fact, newspapers were widely read and were one of the most important sources of information for ordinary people, especially in the area around Turin. Consider that in 1901 only 52 percent of Italians could read and write, but in the Piedmont region 90 percent of the population could read and write—one of the highest literacy rates in the country.

The Catholic press at the time was active, and among other notable newspapers was *Il Giovane Piedmont*, the official newspaper of the Catholic Youth of Piedmont. The weekly review, Conquiste Giovanili, began publication in 1924, but survived only one year, and gave way to *L'Armonia*, the official organ of Catholic Action at the diocesan level. Pier Giorgio supported various periodicals: *Il Popolo* (shut down in April 1924), and the magazine *Il Pensiero Popolare* (published from 1920 to 1923), that was established by Attilio Piccioni. Around the same time, the newspaper *Il Domani d'Italia*, began publishing under the motto, "For the coming of Christ, for the coming of the people." Pier Giorgio liked the motto so much that he helped to cover the paper's publishing costs.

Il Momento was the first truly Catholic daily, established in 1903 at the behest of Turin's archbishop, Agostino Richelmy. But financial troubles in the early 1920s caused the paper to fall into the hands of the pro-Fascist Italian Editorial Union.[38] Pier Giorgio wrote to Antonio Villani:

> I am still trying to make sense of the violence the Communists have caused in some countries; but at least that violence was

> in the name of a larger ideal, namely, to raise the condition of the working class after years of exploitation at the hands of men with no conscience. But what higher ideal do the Fascists have? The vile money paid out by the industrialists and, shamefully, even by our own government, answers only to the logic of the dollar and dishonesty. Fortunately, ultimate justice awaits us in the next life; without a good and fair God, our lives would be useless.[39]

What pained Pier Giorgio most was the adherence of so many Christians to Mussolini's regime; it distressed him to see their error in judgment and their about-face on Fascism, to say nothing of the dangerous and embarrassing willingness of many Church officials to support Mussolini. "It is better to stand alone, but with a clean conscience," Pier Giorgio wrote to Antonio Severi, "than to stand with all the rest, but with a giant stain on our conscience."[40]

In the autumn of 1923, Pier Giorgio resigned from the Cesare Balbo Club. In October of that year, the club marked an official visit by Prime Minister Mussolini to the city by flying its flag in his honor. Pier Giorgio was so angry at the display that he ripped the flag from the balcony and then immediately handed in his resignation from the group. Pier Giorgio wrote to Costantino Guardia-Riva, the president of the club:

> I am truly indignant because the flag which I, unworthy though I am, have carried so often in religious processions,

> was hung by you from the balcony to pay homage to one [Mussolini] who shuts down charitable works [*Opere Pie*], who does not check the Fascists, and allows ministers of God, like Father Minzoni, to be killed, and permits other disgusting crimes to be committed and tries to cover these up by putting a crucifix in schools, etc. I shall, with God's help, continue even outside the club to do what I can for the Christian cause and the peace of Christ.[41]

A month later, upon Guardia-Riva's request, Pier Giorgio withdrew his resignation explaining that in no way did he want others to interpret his action as an "opposition to any one individual, or based on ulterior motives."

A lively and demanding character, Pier Giorgio was without a doubt a sincere militant for the cause in the truest sense. Pier Giorgio was always ready to help even if that meant moving furniture, hanging posters, or sweeping office floors. He was even prepared to face a beating because, as he said, "he who resorts to bullying is the one who should be afraid, not the victim."[42]

One of the chief advocates for Pier Giorgio's beatification, a religious by the name of Gustavo Luigi Furfaro, describes Pier Giorgio as a "wonderful 'Pauline fighter.'" Pier Giorgio, Furfaro says, "was someone who willingly paid a personal price for sincerely questioning things, because he questioned out of love not out of malice. He fought in order to build not to destroy; he struggled to raise things up not to tear them down."[43]

Pier Giorgio always wore the badge of the Catholic Party—the so-called *scudo crociato* or shield of the crusade—though it was dangerous.[44] Perhaps the risk he took in wearing the badge was an act of arrogance on Pier Giorgio's part or an example of exaggerated courage, but the journalist Carlo Trabucco argues that though it might appear "an excessive gesture, [it] does not take away from the beauty of his fervor, which was anything but opportunistic or self-serving."[45]

In truth, Pier Giorgio's love for the poor guided his political choices. Luciana recalls that Pier Giorgio believed that "when the day of a violent political insurrection finally comes, the oppressed will come to Catholics to ask them to explain the support they so readily gave to the strong, the bullies, the immoral ones." Pier Giorgio was convinced that when that day did come, "there had to be at least some Catholics who could hold their heads up high and declare that not all of us are traitors."[46]

As the Frassatis sat down for dinner the evening of June 22, 1924, a group of Fascist hooligans broke into their home. Pier Giorgio showed great courage and presence of mind, and somehow managed to put the ruffians on the run. All the papers reported the incident; which was serious though no one was hurt. Pier Giorgio immediately wrote to Antonio Villani to set his mind at ease:

Dear Tonino,

I'm writing to tell you that you'll be reading in the newspapers about some damage the Fascist pigs did to our

> place. It was the work of cowards, and nothing more. . . . We're lucky that today we can pat ourselves on the back because we have always opposed this party, made up of delinquents, thieves, assassins, or plain idiots. . . .[47]

Pier Giorgio was capable of acting courageously, and he never hesitated to jump into the fray and risk everything for what he believed. When Pier Giorgio learned that Fascist officials were holding Giuseppe Donati, the editor of the newspaper *Il Popolo*, near Turin, he risked arrest to see Donati just to shake his hand and pledge his personal solidarity as well as that of all the members of the Catholic Party. The Frassatis learned of Pier Giorgio's gesture long after his death.

The well known Christian Democrat, social reformer, and peace activist, Giorgio La Pira, once stated that Pier Giorgio's involvement in political and social causes were two sides of the same coin: building up the Kingdom of God. A man of faith living in the world, Pier Giorgio was an active participant in the religious and civil life of his generation. He was a Christian committed to promoting the cause of justice and truth. He used to say, "By the grace of God, I hope to continue down the path of Catholic ideals, so that one day, when and where God wills, I will be able to defend and teach these unique and true ideals."

Pier Giorgio was not afraid to express his opinions, and he did so with great conviction, which sometimes got him into trouble with the law. At the annual meeting of the Young Catholics in September 1921, about 30,000 young people gathered in Rome to meet with Pope Benedict XV in the magnificent Vatican Gardens. After the papal audience, the young people were processing to the Church of Santa Maria in Vallicella. Clashes suddenly broke out between the pilgrims and the police. In an attempt to defend the banner of the Cesare Balbo University Club, Pier Giorgio's was roughed up a bit and the arrested by the police along with many other young people. However, when the police realized that they had detained the son of Alfredo Frassati, they told him he was free to go. However, Pier Giorgio refused and chose instead to remain in jail with his friends until the police released them all.

The next day, during the Mass at Saint Peter's, Pier Giorgio held up the banner that had been tattered in the previous day's scuffle with a placard attached to it that read: "Our flag—slashed by order of the government."

In addition to Pier Giorgio's volunteer work for the Saint Vincent De Paul Society during his years as a university student, he was deeply involved in the activities of Catholic student groups, which were a hotbed of vocations—political and religious.[48] In 1919, Pier Giorgio joined the Federazione Universitaria Cattolici Italiani (Italian Catholic University Federation) or FUCI,[49] an organization affiliated with the Cesare Balbo University Club. Then, in 1920, he joined a university group that occasionally spent evenings in adoration of the Blessed Sacrament, and the "Working Class Youth," a group in Santa Maria in Piazza. Pier Giorgio also attended meetings of non-student groups including the "Savonarola," a club of Catholic workers founded in 1914 by the Dominican priest Father Robotti, under the guidance of Cardinal Richelmy. This was an organization made up almost entirely of metal and mechanical workers from

Turin's main automobile factory, Fiat. Pier Giorgio was active with another group, the Bianchetta, which worked mainly with war veterans, as well as with the "Labor Union," a meeting place for students and workers. It seemed that wherever a group of Catholic youths gathered, Pier Giorgio was sure to be there.

Given the highly individualistic mentality of our times, it might be difficult to understand the appeal of belonging to so many groups. At the time, collective organizations attracted large numbers of young people, mainly university students. However, beginning in 1925, Mussolini's government attempted to curb such organizations. The government presented Italy's parliament with a bill to restrict the freedom of association, using the excuse that it intended to target the so-called secret societies, especially the Free Masons. However, the wording of the legislation left the government free to intervene in the affairs of any sort of organization, professional or working class, with the ultimate aim of suffocating freedom of association. A committed and active member of so many organizations, this legislation certainly affected Pier Giorgio.

Without question, the group that had the most profound influence on Pier Giorgio was the FUCI, a group established by Romolo Murri in 1896. In August 1921, 800 students, including Pier Giorgio, took part in the Tenth Annual Meeting of the FUCI in Ravenna, Italy. During this meeting, Pier Giorgio and some of his friends proposed that the FUCI become a branch of Catholic Youth. The assembly rejected the proposal, in large part because of the opposition of certain Church officials who acted as advisors to the FUCI.

At the heart of all of Pier Giorgio's many activities, which took up most of his time, was a single common denominator: faith. In the Declaration on the Heroic Virtues of Pier Giorgio Frassati, we read, "Christ's love defends liberty and works toward social justice as the logical expression of a Christian understanding of man and the world . . . Pier Giorgio's love is similarly a virtue that animates his political and social commitment."[50]

Indeed, Pier Giorgio's faith infused every aspect of his life, filling it with light and informing his social and political action. When it came to politics, Pier Giorgio was a committed democrat and a staunch anti-Fascist. When it came to social issues, Pier Giorgio's commitment showed itself through a variety of activities, all of them expressions of his Christian faith put into action.

While Pier Giorgio was vocal in his opinions, at the same time he respected the opinions of others, as Marco Beltramo recalled:

> I often noticed how, during even the most heated debates in the Cesare Balbo Club, Pier Giorgio went out of his way to show respect and kindness toward his opponent, as if to show that he was fighting an idea, not the individual.[51]

It never troubled Pier Giorgio to be in the minority or to yield to others if he believed that was the right thing to do. In the winter of 1922, Pier Giorgio and some of his friends from the university tried to protect a bulletin board on which the FUCI posted its announcements. A small group of anti-clerical individuals was attempting to tear down a poster that announced an upcoming all-night adoration of the Blessed

Sacrament. Pier Giorgio knew he was asking for trouble, but he confronted the group just the same. In the end, the bulletin board was torn to pieces, and Pier Giorgio, bruises and all, went home with his head held high.

Chapter 5

Filial Devotion to Mary

About eight kilometers from Pollone, at 1,180 meters above sea level, stands the Church of the Madonna of Oropa, a shrine to the Virgin Mary that attracts thousands of pilgrims and tourists each year. The shrine is home to a wooden statue of the Virgin, which according to tradition Saint Luke the Evangelist carved and Saint Eusebius brought to Piedmont from Jerusalem in the fourth century.

When in Pollone, Pier Giorgio climbed the heights to visit the shrine almost every day. Without his parents' knowledge, Pier Giorgio would wake up before daybreak to bring flowers to "his" Madonna at the shrine in Oropa. With the help of his friend, the faithful gardener, Pier Giorgio devised a system to wake him up without disturbing the rest of the household. The gardener would sound a very special kind of "alarm" consisting of a rope tied on one end to Pier Giorgio's fist, with the other running out of his bedroom window and into the gardener's house. When it was time for Pier Giorgio to rise, the obliging gardener simply tugged on the rope, and it did the trick. Pier Giorgio would jump out of bed, dress in a hurry, grab his backpack and walking stick, and sneak out of the house by a side door. It usually took an hour to walk to the shrine under the star lit sky. Pier Giorgio went to Mass, received Holy Communion, and then prayed at a side-altar before the image of the Madonna. On the way home Pier Giorgio prayed the Rosary aloud, as was his usual custom, and then he would sing the litany of the Blessed Virgin Mary as the sun began rising in the east. As the night gave way to the dawn, Pier Giorgio would feel his spirit soaring and his heart overflowing with love and happiness. He had gone to see and pay homage to "his" Madonna.

Saint Thérèse of Lisieux said that "The perfect expression of the little way in the divine plan is the very life of Mary." In May 1918, Pier Giorgio offered his life to the Virgin Mary: "Oh my sovereign and my Mother, I offer everything to you. And to show you the extent of my devotion, I offer you today, and always, my eyes, my mouth, my heart, my whole being. Because I belong to you, O Mother, keep watch over me, defend me as if I were your own property."

The faith that infused every aspect of Pier Giorgio's life was generous and clear, nurtured and strengthened by a fervent devotion to the Virgin Mary. He prayed the Rosary every day—and not just at home before retiring. He would pray it while riding on streetcars or trains and while walking the city's streets. One day, Pier Giorgio bumped into an acquaintance who was rather surprised to see Pier Giorgio holding a rosary in his hand. He teased, "So, have you become pious now?" Pier Giorgio answered serenely, "No, I have simply remained a Christian."

On May 22, 1922, at the age of twenty-one, Pier Giorgio was received into the Third Order Dominicans and took the name Girolamo, in honor of Savonarola, a man he greatly admired. Savonarola was a Dominican priest who had been burned at the stake in 1498 for his fiery preaching against the widespread corruption in the Church and society. Many university organizations and periodicals of the early twentieth century saw Savonarola as a model of coherence and radical commitment. Some of the Dominican fathers tried to convince Pier Giorgio to choose the name of another canonized or beatified member of the Order. But Pier Giorgio refused to budge.[52]

The story of Savonarola and his energetic struggle against the tyranny of the Medici family fascinated Pier Giorgio, and after becoming a member of the Third Order, he began signing his letters "fra Girolamo." To Antonio Villani, who was also interested in the Dominicans, Pier Giorgio wrote, "I am a fervent admirer of this friar, who died as a saint at the stake. In becoming a tertiary, I wanted to take him as a model, but I am far from being like him."[53]

Pier Giorgio's decision to make this commitment matured over the course of a few years. From the time he first encountered Dominican spirituality in 1918, Pier Giorgio had the time and the opportunity to discern his calling to the life of a lay Dominican. In the Order, he found the way to serve as a witness to the truth in the spirit of that great Spanish saint, Dominic de Guzman, who founded the Order of Preachers (or Dominicans as they came to be more commonly known) in 1215.

In 1923, deeply moved and with tears streaming down his face, Pier Giorgio professed final vows in the Chapel of Our Lady of Grace in Turin's Church of Saint Dominic, with Father Francesco Robotti as his sponsor.

Recalling his visit to Turin in 1922 to celebrate the feast of Saint Dominic, Father Martino Stanislao Gillet, the superior general of the Dominicans at the time, remembered the impression made on him by the small group of university students who had entered as lay members of the Order.

> They were all quite nice, but one in particular really caught my attention as having a special charm. He radiated such kindness that people were drawn to him. His name was Pier Giorgio Frassati.
>
> Pier Giorgio was one of that select group of young people that you find in every university these days, individuals who have a longing for the supernatural, the true sign of an apostle. For him, religion was always a way of life, it was both light and strength, which illuminated and animated all human activity. Nothing was beyond its grasp and, at the same time, it has the power to broaden everything in life.
>
> Pier Giorgio had only time enough to be a student in his short life, but it was clear even then what kind of man he would have been. Not quite an intellectual—that is, someone who dedicates his life to his own philosophy—but rather a man of action, determined to dedicate his philosophy to serving life.[54]

Pier Giorgio had yet another reason to be happy as a member of the Dominican family. Saint Dominic had a profound devotion to the Virgin Mary, and according to tradition, Mary taught Saint Dominic to pray the Rosary. A devout follower of Saint Dominic, Pier Giorgio carried the rosary in his jacket pocket and would take it out at any place, any time, to pray. Pointing to his rosary one day, Pier Giorgio remarked, "I carry my testament in my pocket."[55]

Saints have said that devotion to the Virgin Mary is a sign of predestination, and Pier Giorgio's holiness can only be understood in light of his devotion to Mary, model of the consecrated life and the source of inspiration and guidance for all the saints throughout Church history.

At the Social Institute where Pier Giorgio spent many of his school years, there was a well-established tradition of devotion to the Virgin Mary, going back to 1889 with the establishment of the Marian Congregation. Soon after arriving at the school, Pier Giorgio joined the group, which was then under the spiritual guidance of Father Pietro Lombardi. Pier Giorgio also joined the Society of the Rosary and the Soldiers of Mary, a branch of Catholic Youth based in Turin's Crocetta parish.

Pier Giorgio revealed a strong and sincere love for the Virgin Mary, the love a child feels for his mother. On his bedroom door, Pier Giorgio hung the wonderful prayer of Saint Bernard to the Virgin Mary, found in Dante's *Paradiso*, which he had copied out with great care in his own handwriting.

> Virgin Mother, daughter of thy Son, humble and exalted more than any other creature, fixed goal of the eternal counsel, thou art she who didst so ennoble human nature that its Maker did not disdain to become its creature. In thy womb was rekindled the Love under whose warmth this flower in the eternal peace has thus unfolded. Here thou art for us the

> noonday torch of charity, and below among mortals thou art the living fount of hope. Lady, thou art so great and so availest, that whoso would have grace and has not recourse to thee, his desire seeks to fly without wings. Thy loving-kindness not only succors him who asks, but oftentimes freely foreruns the asking.
>
> In thee is mercy, in thee pity, in thee munificence, in thee is found whatever of goodness is in any creature.[56]

Pier Giorgio would pray these words aloud, followed by the *Salve Regina*—two of his most favorite Marian prayers. Like Dante, Pier Giorgio dreamed of a truly holy Church and loved Mary, the Mother of God, who "most resembles Christ."[57]

Pier Giorgio made a point of praying at the many churches in Turin dedicated to the Virgin Mary. On feast days, he took part in Marian processions and often helped to carry the canopy over the statue of the Virgin Mary through the streets of one of Turin's neighborhoods. It took courage to be publicly involved in a religious procession at that time of great political and social unrest. Religious processions often met with the hostility of both Communists and Fascists, and so being in a procession of the Virgin Mary through the streets of Turin meant risking insult and perhaps even physical harm. Pier Giorgio faced these inevitable confrontations with a resolute and calm heart.

Deeply attached to his friends, Pier Giorgio always remembered them in his prayers at the feet of the Madonna of

Associazione Pier Giorgio Frassati, Rome.

Pier Giorgio, second from right, walking in a procession with the new archbishop of Turin, Bishop Gamba.

Oropa. To Isidoro Bonini, Pier Giorgio wrote, "Tomorrow, as I usually do before leaving Pollone, I'm hiking up to Oropa to pray at the holy sanctuary. I will pray for you at the feet of the Virgin."[58] In October 1924, when Marco Beltramo was leaving to begin his training as a pilot, Pier Giorgio wrote:

> On the twenty-seventh I will be hiking up to Oropa and I will pray for you at the feet of the dark-haired Virgin, for whatever my prayers are worth. As soon as I get back to Turin, I will send you a keepsake: a rosary made from the seeds of some garden plant, to which I will attach a medal of the Madonna of Loreto. May the Virgin Mary watch over you when you "ride with the wind."[59]

Pier Giorgio made rosaries out of the seeds of a plant that grew in the family's garden in Pollone, and he gave these rosaries away as gifts to his friends. It was his way of reminding them of the necessity to pray and of devotion to the Virgin Mary. Years later, Marco Beltramo observed that "The surest means by which Pier Giorgio achieved his union with the Lord, the secret of his spiritual perfection, was his total devotion to Mary."[60]

All the saints progressed toward union with God in the "school" of the Virgin Mary. Saint Louis Mary Grignion de Montfort used to say, "Whenever Mary puts down her roots in a person's soul, one sees the kind of wonders of grace that only she is capable of producing."[61] Through Mary, we come to meet Christ, and through Mary, God seeks to bring us all to holiness.

Chapter 6

Life in the Spirit

One day, Father Righini met Pier Giorgio as he was walking down a street in Turin. They greeted each other and Father Righini asked Pier Giorgio where he was going. Pier Giorgio said he was on his way to the Church of Our Lady of Consolation, but, since they had run into each other, he asked if the priest would hear his confession. The priest agreed and suggested that they go to the nearby Church of the Holy Martyrs. Pier Giorgio insisted that he not go out of his way, "No, no, there is no need to find a church. I can confess my sins right here. . . ." Pier Giorgio immediately took off his cap, made the sign of the cross, and began his confession.

This story, told many years later by Father Righini, captures the essence of Pier Giorgio's spontaneous and open faith; he was respectful, but without being overly formalistic. He never tried to hide his faith, but neither did he take himself too seriously.

During Pope John Paul II's visit to Turin in April 1980, he commented on Pier Giorgio's "response" to Christ.

> Even a quick glance at his life, consumed in just twenty-four years is all you need to understand Pier Giorgio's answer to Jesus Christ: it was the response of a modern youth, open to the problems of his culture, to sports—he was a terrific mountaineer—to social matters, to the authentic values of life; yet he was also a man of deep faith, which was nurtured by the message of the Gospel, a man with a solid character, passionate about serving others, and consumed by a deep sense of charity which led him to approach . . . the poor and the sick. . . .
>
> He was a young man whose joy was overflowing, a joy that helped him to overcome the many challenges of his life, challenges all young people face at that time of life.

Pier Giorgio's "overflowing" joy was the fruit of his interior life, and, in the words of Edith Stein, the interior life is a person's deepest, purest source of joy. To look at Pier Giorgio's everyday life is to discover the secrets of his interior life, which is ultimately at the heart of all holiness.

Every morning, while the rest of his family was still asleep, Pier Giorgio quietly slipped out of the house to walk to the nearby church to receive Communion. He was always composed, absorbed in prayer and adoration. As Luciana later recalled, Pier Giorgio "gave great importance to his bearing in church, and even when he passed in front of a church, he would greet his Lord with the most polite bow."[62] The prevailing mood of that era was one of respect toward the human rather than the divine; indeed to make the sign of the cross in public or to remove one's hat in front of a church as a sign of respect could be dangerous. This did not stop Pier Giorgio from boldly making his solemn signs of the cross.

"Behold," says the Book of Revelation, "I stand at the door and knock. If anyone hears my voice and opens the door, then I will enter his house and dine with him, and he with me" (3:20). Pier Giorgio perceived the Lord knocking at the door of his heart and opened his life wide to God's presence. Pier Giorgio had had to discover his faith on his own, and it was a discovery made in solitude and silence with God as his friend. What Pier Giorgio discovered was not an abstract idea of a distant God, but a real person, a God made flesh in the person of Jesus Christ. For Pier Giorgio, faith became the very reason for life itself, and he nourished this faith day to day with his tireless reading of Sacred Scripture and with the Eucharist. Thanks to the formation he received from the Jesuits, Pier Giorgio developed a Christ-centered and sacramental spirituality, which meant he availed himself of the sacrament of Reconciliation frequently (at least three times a week), and daily reception of the Eucharist.

Pier Giorgio belonged to a group of young people devoted to participating in all-night adoration of the Blessed Sacrament, choosing to spend the precious few hours they had for much-needed sleep in prayer. During one such all-night vigil in the cathedral of Turin, Pier Giorgio became so absorbed in prayer and adoration that he did not notice that one of the large candles nearby was dripping hot wax onto his head and neck. When Pier Giorgio prayed, it seemed as if silence enveloped him completely and he became immersed in what Saint Teresa of Avila called "the infinite sea of the divine

Truth."[63] The Eucharist gave Pier Giorgio the strength and happiness to live each day. He once said of his devotion to the Eucharist, "After a prayer vigil, I feel stronger, safer, more secure, and even happier."[64]

Pier Giorgio understood that "to adore was the greatest act," because it meant taking part in the life of the saints in heaven, something he had learned from priests of the Congregation of the Most Blessed Sacrament, through whom he came to know the thought and spirituality of their founder, Saint Peter Julian Eymard, the great believer in and preacher of Eucharistic devotion. Cardinal Giovanni Saldarini said of Pier Giorgio's profound Eucharistic devotion, "he was a Eucharistic Christian, and, as such, he was passionate about charity. . . . For him, the Eucharist was more than a parenthesis in the midst of everyday life, rather it was the very heart of his existence; without this commitment, it would be impossible to build a truly Eucharistic life, that is, a life of gratitude and openness, a life that recognizes and is thankful for blessings, a life that gives of itself without hesitation to everyone and to anyone."

Pier Giorgio's deepest desires found perfect expression in the motto of Catholic Action: *Action, prayer, and sacrifice*. Pier Giorgio was active yet contemplative, idealistic yet concrete, utopian yet pragmatic. Pier Giorgio was a contemplative even in his action. The true secret of his spiritual life was prayer, through which he realized a mystical union with God. In prayer, Pier Giorgio found the fulfillment of Jesus' words: "Those who drink of the water that I will give them will never be thirsty. The water that I will give will become in them a spring of water gushing up to eternal life." (Jn 4:14)

No matter how busy he was, Pier Giorgio found the time to pray. At night, he would fall asleep in prayer; and in the morning, he woke up early in order to pray. His prayer was so intense that it seemed to carry him away, and those who knew him never forgot the impression made on them as they watched Pier Giorgio in prayer.

Pier Giorgio felt especially attached to reading and meditating on the letters of Saint Paul, which he often urged his friends to read. He copied Paul's famous hymn of love from the first letter to the Corinthians—"love is patient, love is kind . . ."—and kept it on his desk so that it was always before his eyes. Pier Giorgio was also quite familiar with the works of Saint Augustine and had a particular fondness for his Confessions. In December 1924, Pier Giorgio wrote to Marco Beltramo:

> I want to follow the straight and narrow path, but with every step I trip and fall; that is why I ask you to pray for me whenever you can, until, God willing, I reach the end of the difficult but straight and narrow path. In any event, these days I am mixing my rather boring studies with the marvelous writings of Saint Augustine; never before have I found such endless enjoyment, because in reading Augustine's powerful Confessions, we get a glimpse of the joy reserved for those who die under the sign of the cross.[65]

Pier Giorgio also nurtured a special devotion to the writings of Saint Catherine of Siena, also a member of the Third Order Dominicans. When Luciana graduated from university, Pier Giorgio gave her a book about the saint from Siena as a gift so that, as he wrote in his dedication, Saint Catherine might be a guide for his sister "along the path toward Christian perfection." In fact, Pier Giorgio was reading the life of Saint Catherine just days before he died, and it lay open next to his bed.

The twentieth-century martyr of Auschwitz, Saint Maximilian Kolbe, once observed that "it is a false, though widespread, assumption that the saints were very different than we are." What distinguishes the saints is their great docility to the Holy Spirit's power, which opens the door to divine grace through the hidden, silent, tireless work of interior conversion. "It is the spirit that gives life; the flesh is useless" (Jn 6:63).

Throughout the ages, saints have been completely receptive to the work of the Holy Spirit in their lives, and Pier Giorgio was open to the power of the Spirit in an amazing way. According to Dan Montgomery, a Christian psychologist, believers can see the mysterious Third Person of the most Holy Trinity as "an artesian well that springs from deep within us."[66] It is like a spring that is invisible to the eyes, but visible to the heart, that flows from our souls into that which we can define as our spiritual core.

What psychologists refer to as a person's "core" or "self," Scripture calls the "heart." As Montgomery puts it, "Our spiritual core reflects the fact that we are created in the image of God and that we know him intimately."[67] Our "spiritual core," that is to say the very essence of our being, is the source of the individuality and uniqueness God has given us and is itself proof of Christ's presence in each of us. The living water of which Jesus speaks in the Gospel of John (cf. 7:38) is none other than the Holy Spirit, the inner Teacher who shapes our spirit and, in the words of Saint John Vianney, the Curé of Ars, "is like a gardener, [who] cultivates our soul." This is a fitting image for the Holy Spirit. Just as a gardener trims plants, removes wilted growth, and pulls up weeds, the Holy Spirit tends those who are open to his guidance.

Pier Giorgio Frassati's expansive and cheerful disposition, his youthful exuberance, and his sincere and straightforward manner—without a trace of a holier-than-thou attitude—all reflected a perfect balance of his gifts of mind and heart. His life clearly reveals what it means for one to allow God to act directly on one's personality.

Happiness is the first duty of every Christian, the first tool of discipleship. Pier Giorgio made happiness his banner. Luciana described Pier Giorgio's religious devotion as being neither "severe, nor disagreeable, nor inaccessible; he was peaceful and happy not only by nature, but also because he achieved this state through his interior life."[68] Always smiling, with a kind word for everyone, Pier Giorgio knew how to be strong yet delicate, loyal and sincere, exuberant but self-controlled, serious and deeply committed in his personal relationships. He had a subtle sense of humor and was completely generous and available to anyone he met. Pier Giorgio was not a rigid individual, nor was he unilateral in his actions. Rather, he was a harmonious and open-minded person. The action of grace carved his personality and the Holy Spirit molded him. Indeed, the Holy Spirit, which flows like a spring from the depths our souls, is the key to a balanced and well-rounded personality.

> Life according to the Spirit, whose fruit is holiness (cf. Rom 6:22; Gal 5:22), stirs up every baptized person and requires

This photo captures Pier Giorgio's physical strength and reflective nature.

> each to follow and imitate Jesus Christ in embracing the beatitudes; in listening and meditating on the Word of God; in conscious and active participation in the liturgical and sacramental life of the Church; in personal prayer; in family or in community; in the hunger and thirst for justice; in the practice of the commandment of love in all circumstances of life and service to the brethren, especially the least, the poor and the suffering.[69]

The Fathers of the Church use the word *filocalia*—that is, love for divine beauty which radiates from divine love—to describe the spiritual journey toward purity under the guidance of the Holy Spirit in the hopes of daily becoming people who live "in the image of Christ."

Pier Giorgio was one of those who daily worked to become better conformed to the image of Christ. He was a man energized by his faith and purified by his love for others. He knew how to be silent and intensely prayerful, and how to be joyous and bright with his friends. He was able to balance his enthusiasm with prudence, his discipline with the youthful spirit of a university student. His emblem was his happiness, the fruit of the Holy Spirit. To him, as to all of us, Jesus said, "The kingdom of God is among you" (Lk 17:21). And in his letter to the Romans, Saint Paul wrote: "For the Kingdom of God is not food and drink but righteousness and peace and joy in the Holy Spirit" (14:17).

The Holy Spirit, the "sweet host of the soul" that rested within Pier Giorgio inspired him to become a witness to the Kingdom of God, revealed to him as he followed the ways of Jesus Christ in peace and joy. It was a journey "filled with many thorns, but also with many roses."[70]

Chapter 7

Seeing Christ in the Poor

Pier Giorgio Frassati was a man dedicated to social action, a commitment deeply rooted in the Piedmont tradition of "social saints"—individuals like Joseph Cottolengo, Joseph Cafasso, and John Bosco, who were models of hardworking and concrete forms of charity and social action performed with heart in hand without frills or preferences. In the Gospel, Jesus tells his disciples that "many who are first will be last, and the last will be first" (Mt 19:30). Pier Giorgio was a rich young man, who was able to put "the last" first in his life and devoted himself to the poor and needy, understanding that the least of our brothers and sisters on this earth are first in God's heart.

One of Pier Giorgio's classmates related the following incident.

> As I was returning home one afternoon in February 1924, I bumped into Pier Giorgio on the street as he walked hurriedly by with a large package under his arm. We both

> stopped, and, with a smile on my face, I asked where he was going in such a rush and with such a large package; truth be told, my question was a bit indiscreet, but I asked it without much thought. Pier Giorgio looked at me hesitantly for a moment, but then, with his usual affectionate warmth, he said: "Do you want to come with me? I'm going to Cottolengo.[71] They told me to bring this package and to distribute some things; you can help me."
>
> And so, for the first time I went with him to that place where the most awful and gloomy human suffering had found a refuge and a helping hand. Seeing how these forsaken people welcomed Pier Giorgio, and how much comfort they found in his visit, I realized then and there just who had brought the packages and those items to be handed out. I also understood it was not the first time. In fact, Pier Giorgio regularly used his own savings to bring material comfort and help to the poor, while his very presence among them was like a ray of light. While I waited outside, Pier Giorgio insisted on continuing his visit on his own, and he went inside to visit the lodgings where the horror and the misery of human poverty was at its worst. When he came out, Pier Giorgio seemed like someone who had come back from another world, another life. On his face, emotional and transformed, you could see that bright light of spirituality that must have shone on the face of the saints. Standing next to him, I felt somehow smaller, yet also more human and more kind.[72]

There is nothing surprising in this touching recollection of Pier Giorgio, who as a child put aside his allowance to send to missionaries, who as a teenager would encourage readers of *La Stampa* to tend to the needs of the poor, and as a young man spent what little spare time he had, even in the midst of his studies, to visit the poor.

When Pier Giorgio turned twenty-four on April 6, 1925, his father gave him a generous cash gift, which Pier Giorgio promptly used to purchase furniture for the Saint Vincent de Paul Society at the Legion of Mary Club. On another occasion, Alfredo Frassati, in view of his son's near completion of his university studies, offered Pier Giorgio the choice of a graduation gift: he could have a new car or, if he preferred, the value of that car in cash—certainly a considerable sum in those days. Pier Giorgio did not hesitate. Though a car was a cherished status symbol at the time, Pier Giorgio chose the gift of cash, which, as he confided to a friend, would allow him to better help "his" poor.

Italia Nebbia was a witness to Pier Giorgio's generous charity.

> I owned a small convenience store on Vercelli Street. One day, two young men stopped in front of the store in an open carriage filled with bags and packages. Curious, I went out to have a look. I noticed that one of the two men would come down from the carriage and gather up a load of these packages, and disappear every now and then. He sometimes returned with a bag in hand. It was then that he entered my shop for the first time, and explained that the people for whom the packages were intended were not at home. He asked me if I would deliver them just as soon as they returned. I readily agreed, since each package was clearly marked for the appropriate destination. From then on, whenever no one was at home to receive the packages that young man would leave these with me. Since he struck me

> as someone you could talk to, I asked him one day, "You are dressed so well you look like a true gentleman, yet you go around with these sacks. What will people say? Why don't you let me deliver them since I'm a shopkeeper and people won't think twice about it?" He answered, "No, really, I'm so happy when I find these people at home . . . I prefer to deliver the packages personally, because that way I can also encourage them a bit, give them hope that their lives will change, and above all I can convince them to offer their sufferings to God and to go to Mass."

The young man's words hit home. Italia Nebbia never went to Mass, and she admitted this to Pier Giorgio. "If you won't go for yourself," he said to her, "then at least go for the sake of your child." The shopkeeper was so struck by his words that she changed her life.

> I told him he was absolutely right. In fact, I went to Mass the very next Sunday. Never in my life had I heard a good word. I was orphaned when I was only three years old. I was struck by the explanation of the Gospel. And so it was that for the first time since I was married, I started going to Mass. I told that young man when I saw him again, and I even repeated the sermon on the Gospel. I had the sense that he understood that all I needed was a few words of faith. Then he asked me to share a few of these good words with the people to whom I delivered the packages. He had found a way to teach me these words, so that I would learn them for myself and be able to share them with others.[73]

Pier Giorgio Frassati's work on behalf of the Saint Vincent de Paul Society was diligent and tireless despite his academic responsibilities and the time he devoted to sports and to friends. Someone once commented that "the boundless generosity with which Pier Giorgio gave himself to others, truly giving them his all, was the result of a process of deep, internal maturation, a stage Pier Giorgio reached very quickly, living fully and completely in God and placing all his trust in him. That is, Pier Giorgio came to understand that man fulfills his very nature, sanctifies himself, only to the extent that he opens himself up to God's gift."[74]

Often Pier Giorgio would stay at the bedside of a sick person well into the night. Alfredo Frassati, whose work at the newspaper usually kept him out until after midnight, was in the habit of checking on his son to be sure he was sound asleep. Once, when Alfredo discovered that Pier Giorgio had not yet come home, he waited for him. When Pier Giorgio came in well after midnight, Alfredo asked why he could not have at least called home to tell his family he would be coming home late. Pier Giorgio answered simply, "Because where I was they had no phone."

One observer wrote this commentary on the life of Pier Giorgio:

> [He] was someone who thought and acted in the freedom and sovereignty of the Spirit: on the one hand, shaking off the yoke of wealth, he liberates himself from the falsehood of the bourgeois lifestyle and gives his life a mark of generosity foreign to all selfishness. On the other hand, he uses his wealth not to satisfy his whims or honest needs, but to

do good always and everywhere for those in need. Pier Giorgio declares in a loud voice that true happiness is to be found elsewhere.[75]

Pier Giorgio truly was "poor in spirit." He saved everything for the poor and kept nothing for himself. When he traveled by train, he always went third class because, as he liked to say, there was no fourth. If he happened upon a needy person on the street, he would stop to listen to them first and then empty his pockets into that individual's hands. One cold winter day a friend met Pier Giorgio walking along the street wearing only a light blazer. "Aren't you cold?" the friend asked him. "Oh, no," Pier Giorgio quickly answered, "you know I'm a mountaineer!" His casual manner and light-hearted remark hid the fact that he had just given away his coat to a freezing beggar. Truly, Pier Giorgio showed through his actions that he believed that in serving the homeless, the naked, the hungry, he was serving Christ who said: "Truly I tell you, just as you did [this] to one of the least of these who are members of my family, you did it to me" (Mt 25:40).

Whenever Pier Giorgio entered the miserable lodgings of those he helped, he would respectfully take off his cap, offer his hand in a warm gesture, and show the utmost courtesy and concern. He never told anyone who he was, but simply introduced himself as a member of the Saint Vincent de Paul Society. He never used the family's car, but reached the poorer areas of the city by foot or public transportation, loaded down with sacks and packages.

Pier Giorgio was careful to "consult" the family cook when he prepared packages for the poor. He asked advice on how much food a family of four, six, or eight would need, and exactly what kinds of food children needed for proper nourishment. He often asked the family's servants to gather clothes for the poor. Not only did he insist that these items of clothing be in good condition, but also washed and ironed. "One shouldn't give rags to the poor," Pier Giorgio would say firmly.

Pier Giorgio's love and care for "the poor" was not directed toward a general group; he loved and cared for the individuals he met, seeing in each person the very face of Christ. He said, "I see a special light around the sick, the poor, the less fortunate, a light that we do not possess."[76] Pier Giorgio's life is a concrete expression of unity between faith and actions, a unity difficult even for practicing Christians to achieve.

Pier Giorgio never looked upon another as a stranger, but as a person to identify with to the point of taking on his or her burdens. He never delegated the care of the poor to others, and he never simply opened his wallet to help those in need. Instead, he gave of himself. His charitable actions were not a handout, but an act of true solidarity; not a performance of false piety, but the love of God in action. He used to say, "Jesus comes to me every day in Communion, and I return the visit by going to serve the poor."[77]

Indeed, Pier Giorgio's love of neighbor, created in the image of God, sprang from the Eucharist. For Pier Giorgio, faith was not a personal possession or interior refuge, but a dynamic and concrete force that impelled him to do for others in the name of Love. This force was born of prayer and the Eucharist. Eucharistic adoration refined Pier Giorgio's heart and made it possible for him to give his heart to others. In fact, charity without prayer would not be true charity, but mere philanthropy or generic kindness.

Even when Pier Giorgio felt overwhelmed with his studies, he refused to put aside his work with the poor. Every week he visited four or five families and brought not only material assistance in the form of coupons with which to buy bread for the week, or clothing, blankets, medicine, firewood and coal for heating, but also, and above all, spiritual support. He took advantage of his visits to distribute copies of the Gospel or of the book *The Imitation of Christ*, urging the poor to pray, to go to Mass, and to draw nearer to the sacraments. He did all of this without prejudice and without moralizing. "As a perfect disciple of Christ," Italo Alighiero Chiusano wrote, "Pier Giorgio loved human beings one by one, face by face, name by name, each person with his own unique voice, his own heavy breathing, his own wrinkles, his own bad mood."[78]

In December 1922, Pier Giorgio suddenly quit the Saint Vincent de Paul Society of the Institute run by the Jesuits. Members of the group refused to help a family in need because of the "bad behavior" of one family member. Commenting on the matter to his friend, Carlo Bellingieri, Pier Giorgio wrote:

> If you want my opinion, I would do away with certain groups of the Saint Vincent de Paul Society. When they have people living in another time, and so filled with Christian zeal, yet do not even know enough to warn parents of the supposed conduct of their children and try to help the situation, but instead prefer to simply abandon that family, it would be better if the group did not exist at all not

> because these people act in bad faith, but because they do not adapt to modern times.[79]

Pier Giorgio's charity was unconditional. He did not pass judgment on anyone; he did not need to know if the people he helped had a police record; he did not ask questions to find out if they agreed with his way of thinking. People were poor and they needed help; that was all that mattered to Pier Giorgio. They were the poor whom he was called to love with the heart of Christ.

Chapter 8

Ascending the Heights

At the beginning of the twentieth century, spectator sports as a means of weekend entertainment were not the mass phenomenon we know today. Rather, at least in Italy, weekend trips to the mountains were the rage. With far-sightedness, the Catholic world understood the educational value of sports, as seen in the establishment of the National Catholic Sports Federation in 1906. What is more, in 1922, the Archbishop of Milan, Achille Ratti, became Pope Pius XI. In his youth, the new pope had nurtured such a great passion for mountaineering that people had dubbed him the "Alpine pope."

Pier Giorgio Frassati also felt a great attraction to mountains and joined the Italian Alpine Club. Though he played other sports well, mountain climbing had a special place in his heart. He took his first trip to the mountains with his mother, who was interested in painting the landscape, when he was six or seven years old. His love for mountain heights remained with him until his death.

Pier Giorgio considered his mountain excursions both a physical challenge and spiritual joy.

Associazione Pier Giorgio Frassati, Rome.

The skilled climber and athlete, Pier Giorgio, in a mountain descent, 1923.

Pier Giorgio joined the organization, "Mountain Youth," that was established in 1914 by a group of young Catholics whose aim was to emphasize the spiritual aspect of mountaineering. The organization paid special attention to festive celebrations that accompanied their excursions.

Mountains symbolized the bridge between heaven and earth and Pier Giorgio saw them as a unique place to meet God and come face to face with the mystery of creation itself. The effort to scale a mountain peak meant more than physical exercise to Pier Giorgio; every climb strengthened both his body and his spirit. His mountain excursions inspired in him true spiritual joy, and Pier Giorgio desired to share this joy with others. So he organized trips to the mountains and invited his closest friends to accompany him. Just as the sun began to rise, he and his companions would set out, ropes and ice axes in hand and a sack of food slung over their shoulders. Pier Giorgio was hardly still for a moment on a trip up a mountain, encouraging his companions, entertaining them with jokes, and taking care of their every need. He would whistle as if he were a stationmaster to stop his companions in order to offer them something to eat or drink, and create such a spectacle that his companions would break up with laughter.

Shortly after his death, one of his companions, Clementina Luotto, recalled the mountain excursions and the joy that Pier Giorgio brought to them in a touching letter.

> Now who will go to the mountains again? Do you remember [Pier Giorgio's] overcoat? And those minerals that he carried—for a microbe of garnet, we said, and he laughed and sparkled with joy. And his whistle to call to those who

Pier Giorgio *(center with rope)* on a hiking trip with fellow students and members of FUCI (the Federation of Italian Catholic University Students).

> were far behind? And what about those meals? From sweet, to salty, to acidic, only to go back to sweet, and then salty again ... And Tina would say to him: "But Frassati, you will make us lose our appetites!" And he would apologize as if he were guilty of some great fault and offered us everything he had with that deep voice of his and generous gesture which, for those who knew him, will always seem the very image of cordiality, now gone for good. ...[80]

As Clementina Luotto mentioned in her letter, Pier Giorgio always returned from his mountain trips laden with rocks. From his childhood, Pier Giorgio had a passion for mineralogy, and, after every excursion, his coat would serve as a sack for his precious minerals, which he diligently catalogued by their Latin names for his collection.

Pier Giorgio also loved photography. He took dozens of pictures of the incredible mountain scenery he contemplated during those hours of bliss. His friends recalled his contagious energy in the mountain snow where Pier Giorgio's carefree nature and overwhelming cheerfulness brought joy to the entire climbing party. Pier Giorgio also insisted on singing, though he was usually terribly out of tune. He sang with a powerful voice that made everyone laugh. Pier Giorgio's fondness for playing practical jokes made him the life of the party.

Once when Pier Giorgio and his friends were on their way to Oulx (a city between the Bardonecchia Valley and Cesana), bad weather forced the train to stop. With only his trench coat on, Pier Giorgio gave the railway men a hand with carrying luggage, and he walked back and forth the length of the train reciting verses of his favorite poetry. When Pier Giorgio returned to his compartment, his friends complained about the situation. He settled down in his seat and was so quiet that the others thought he had fallen asleep, but he was actually praying the Rosary. He then urged his friends to eat something so that they would not become sick. For his part, Pier Giorgio did not eat because he planned to participate in the celebration of the Eucharist when they reached the summit.

Pier Giorgio never missed Sunday Mass, even if it meant risking being late in joining his friends on a train bound for another mountain trip. Sometimes, having rushed from church to the station, Pier Giorgio arrived just as the train whistle blew and was about to depart.

Every so often, after a climb, he and his friends would go to Mass in the mountains. Without a sign of exhaustion, Pier Giorgio would prepare the altar and serve Mass with concentrated attention and solemnity. "The exuberance of the life of the party and monastic concentration were expressions of the very same spiritual disposition: be it on the mountain peaks or at the feet of the Tabernacle, [Pier Giorgio's] transparent soul encountered God with similar ease."[81]

The mountains—so majestic, remote, and austere—helped to foster Pier Giorgio's spirituality. The mere thought of the mountains became an immediate inspiration for Pier Giorgio to contemplate God. In August 1923, Pier Giorgio wrote to Marco Beltramo, "Every day that passes I fall more and more in love with the mountains; if it weren't for my studies, I would spend entire days up in the pure mountain air, contemplating the greatness of the Creator."[82] To climb to the summit of a mountain in the early morning light, to find there a cross, a religious image, a tiny church, was enough to fill Pier Giorgio with pure delight and inspiration. He often said, "These mountain climbs possess a strange magic so that no matter how many times one repeats them or how similar they may seem, they are never tedious in the same way the eternal and perpetual wonder of spring is never tedious."[83]

Pier Giorgio always found ways to be of service to his companions. He would grease their boots, help those who were short of breath or less skilled, or make some excuse to stop in order to give those who had fallen behind a chance to catch up with the party. At night, after an exhausting climb, the party would lodge in a room so cold that everything—even their clothes—was frozen. Pier Giorgio's companions would retire immediately, without even undressing, while he would kneel on the icy floor to pray the Rosary.

In May 1924, during a trip to Pian della Musa Mountain, Pier Giorgio and some of his friends founded the "The Shady Characters Society," as a way to bind together the young Catholics who shared a love for mountain climbing. Each member was dubbed a "charlatan" and given an appropriate nickname. Pier Giorgio became "Citizen Robespierre," and Marco Beltramo "Perrault," after the character in a play Pier Giorgio had seen. Isidoro Bonini was known as the "Commendator Regina Coeli" (Commander of the Prison in Rome), Franz Massetti became "Petronius Arbiter Elegantiarum" (after the famous member of Nero's court), Clementina Luotto was "L'Irma Gramatica dalla frase ben tornita" (after the famous Italian actress Irma Grammatica), and Ernestina Bonelli "L'englesina" (the English). Laura Hidalgo served as secretary of this happy "organization," which included an internal section of "Terror" led by none other than Pier Giorgio, the "holy terror," with the assistance of Marco Beltramo. This "office" charged them with the task of planning practical jokes against their "co-citizens."

However lighthearted the nature of The Shady Characters Society with its outings and parties seemed, the deeper foundation of the group was the true friendship they shared. The members helped each other, listened to each other's problems, and offered each other advice; they prayed for one another, and shared their anxieties, problems, faith, and love.

Clearly, the presence of friends was very important to Pier Giorgio. He loved having people around and he believed profoundly in the importance of friendship. Just two months before he died, Pier Giorgio wrote to his dearest friend, Marco Beltramo:

> In our earthly life, next to the love of parents and siblings, one of the best expressions of affection is friendship. Every day, I thank God for giving me such good friends, who are a precious guide for my life.[84]

Pier Giorgio also said, "We believe that even when we reach the tomb, the 'shady characters' will remember each other in prayer."

The students belonging to FUCI were Pier Giorgio's closest friends. Through continual correspondence, they formed a strong bond that added substance to the time they spent

Pier Giorgio *(fourth from the left)*, and the members of the "Shady Characters Society," in which he had the "office" of playing practical jokes (1924).

A constant source of fun, Pier Giorgio *(front, second from left)* pulling a keg of wine with his friends (Turin, 1925).

Associazione Pier Giorgio Frassati, Rome.

Always known as the life of the party, Pier Giorgio *(farthest right)* enjoying the company of his friends.

together. Correspondence enriched their relationship in a truly spiritual way. Carlo Bellingieri, Marco Beltramo, Franz Massetti, Isidoro Bonini, Gian Maria Bertini, Antonio Villani, Antonio Severi, Clementina Luotto, Laura Hidalgo, and Ernestina Bonelli all received letters from Pier Giorgio. Indeed, they have preserved and jealously guarded hundreds of letters written by Pier Giorgio. They are letters full of human warmth and affection, and they are rich with details of the times and the things Pier Giorgio and his friends saw and did. Pier Giorgio wrote on just about every subject, whether important issues or small details, including, for example, a pasta recipe he sent to Maria Fischer of Vienna in December 1921.

Pier Giorgio's letters offer a precious record of his earthly life. They are a kind of mirror of his soul that help us to understand his life and the many dimensions of his character and allow us to know him personally. He wrote in a simple but direct style, somewhat like a telegram, often without punctuation. Yet, he was extremely articulate in his communication, employing a lively, humorous tone, and always ending with the same closing: "Saluti in G. C." (Greetings in Jesus Christ). His correspondence was Pier Giorgio's personal way of giving himself to his friends. Taken together, his letters represent a true anthem to friendship lived in the light of love and of a shared faith in God.

Two years after his death, Laura Hidalgo reflected, with a profound sense of regret at his loss, on Pier Giorgio's significance to their circle of friends and fellow believers.

> Now we know because we have mourned him so much, because we still feel him with us even after two years, which

> seem like two hundred since he left us. We know because the trips we took with him were the happiest, because never before or since did nature itself seem to us as majestic and as pure as when we admired it together with him; because his practical jokes had a special scent of youthful happiness. He always placed God as the tie that bound us all together, and in God's name, he blessed our friendship, our joy, our every feeling, and every moment of life.[85]

To celebrate his graduation from university, Pier Giorgio planned to climb Mount Cervino—this was his dream, a long-cherished secret he kept in his heart awaiting the completion of his studies. However, Pier Giorgio's studies were becoming more challenging and difficult to deal with. Writing to Luciana at the end of March 1925, he announced with disappointment, "Now there will be no mountains for a while, so I will have to be happy just greeting them from my window. But how can one resist the temptation of the snow?"[86]

In his short lifetime, Pier Giorgio Frassati completed some forty-four mountain climbs—thirty-nine of them during the last four years! Pope John Paul II noted, "For every one of his mountain hikes, [Pier Giorgio] had drawn up an itinerary to accompany his ascetic and spiritual trip, a school of prayer and adoration." For Pier Giorgio, nature was the place where God's smile was reflected everywhere. He would say, "I understand this desire for the sun, to climb high, to go up and find God at the top."[87]

His last mountain trip, just a month before his death, was to the Lunelle Mountain at Val di Lanzo. There is a beautiful picture of Pier Giorgio at the very top of the mountain, a sense of joy emanating from every pore of his body. The words he wrote at the bottom of the photograph now seem prophetic: Toward Heaven.

Chapter 9

A Secret Love

On one of his many mountain excursions, Pier Giorgio fell in love with Laura Hidalgo, one among his close-knit group of friends. Laura was born on Piccolo San Bernardo Mountain in February 1898. The daughter of a Spanish government official, she was a mathematics student at Turin's Polytechnic University. Laura belonged to Turin's Gaetana Agnesi—named after the famous mathematician and woman of faith—a Catholic university club for women equivalent to the men's Cesare Balbo Club.

Laura was not an exceptionally pretty woman, but she was kindhearted and rich in faith; and she loved the mountains as much as Pier Giorgio. Having lost both her parents, Laura showed great courage in raising her younger brother while working and studying at the same time.

Pier Giorgio fell head over heels in love with Laura Hidalgo, and he dreamed of making her his life-long companion, but so many things stood in the way. Laura was a typical girl belonging to Catholic Action, the kind Pier

Giorgio's parents would certainly have looked down upon and judged unworthy to marry their only son. They dreamed of seeing Pier Giorgio married to someone belonging to Turin's upper class. Unsure of what to do, Pier Giorgio went to speak with Father Antonio Cojazzi, his former tutor.

"Does your mother know how you feel?" the priest asked.

"She doesn't know a thing," Pier Giorgio answered. "She would not be at all pleased, and I know she and Father would be strongly opposed."

"So you're telling me that standing between you and this girl is your parents' wishes. Have you thought about ignoring them?" Father Cojazzi asked.

"No! Never, not under any circumstance," Pier Giorgio responded.

"I feel I should point out that in good conscience you have every right to ignore your parents' opinion, since you're an adult," the priest continued.

"I realize I have that right," Pier Giorgio answered, "but I don't feel I should exercise it."

"Well then," concluded the Salesian priest, "you have no choice but to renounce your feelings for her."

Pier Giorgio lowered his head, his characteristic gesture of agreement, and began to weep. The same young man well known for his courage for refusing to be intimidated by any challenge or to lose heart in the face of disappointment now found himself with his back against a wall.

To test his mother's reaction, Pier Giorgio arranged to have Laura and two other young women over to the house for tea. Not surprisingly, neither Adelaide nor Luciana was impressed. While Pier Giorgio said nothing, he suffered enormously. In a letter to her fiancé, the Polish diplomat, Jan Gawronski, Luciana spoke of Pier Giorgio's pain.

> Last evening, Pier Giorgio came to me with those big black eyes of his and told me he was in love with a young lady, whom I know. . . . Poor boy, it was touching to hear him. . . . I told him it was best if he stopped seeing her, and he assured me he already had. Giorgio also told me that not only did he not mention his feelings to the girl, he never even hinted at it.[88]

Though Pier Giorgio had spent much time with Laura on many mountains trips with their mutual friends, as well as in their volunteer work, he never revealed the nature of his feelings. Actually, few friends ever knew or guessed that Pier Giorgio was in love with Laura. Pier Giorgio kept it a secret and suffered his heartache in silence.

Isidoro Bonini was one friend who did know of Pier Giorgio's suffering. In five letters written between December 1924 and March 1925, Pier Giorgio shared his secret with his dear and trustworthy friend. "Oh, my dear Isidoro," he wrote, "each day that passes I become more convinced how ugly this world is."[89]

Only faith, Pier Giorgio said, could help him in the state he was in and, realizing the power of prayer, he asked his friend to pray for him so that he could more easily "kill the seed"[90] of this silent and undeclared love. On January 29, 1925, Pier Giorgio wrote, "Today, in the struggle, I can only thank God, who in his infinite mercy desires to give me this heartache, so that through these difficulties I might return to a more spiritual interior life."[91]

With an air of detachment, Pier Giorgio sent Laura a bouquet of flowers from Cogne, because, as he wrote, "the Abbot Henry says that young ladies are like flowers and so I would imagine that like creatures would love each other."[92] Without so much as a hint of the turmoil that tore at his heart, he gave Laura a gift: a volume containing one of his favorite parts of Scripture: the Epistles of Saint Paul.

Writing to Isidoro Bonini, Pier Giorgio tried to put his feelings for Laura Hidalgo in spiritual terms.

> My plan now is to transform that special feeling I had for her, but that cannot lead to anything, to the end toward which we must all strive: a respectful bond of Christian friendship, respect for her many virtues, imitation of her outstanding gifts, just as I do with the other girls. Perhaps you will tell me that it is mad for me to hope that this is even possible; but I believe, if you pray for me a little, that I can achieve this goal. . . . This is my plan, which I hope with God's grace to follow, and even if it costs me the sacrifice of my earthly life; it does not matter.[93]

While we cannot know all of the reasons for Pier Giorgio's decision, one obstacle was surely the escalating tension between his parents. Alfredo and Adelaide Frassati's marriage was falling into such an abyss of misunderstanding and spite that a separation seemed inevitable. Pier Giorgio would not allow himself to consider a marriage his parents would certainly oppose and thus place a greater strain on an already fragile relationship. When Father Cojazzi spoke with Pier Giorgio about the difficult situation, he remembers Pier Giorgio telling him: "To destroy one family in order to create another would be absurd and is not even worth thinking about. I will pay the price, but God's will be done."[94]

Here was the same young man who had once called someone an "imbecile" for agreeing to marry a woman his father had chosen. Now, faced with his parents' disintegrating marriage, Pier Giorgio's pure and generous heart led him to say, "I will pay the price."

To make an already painful period of his life worse, in January 1925 Luciana married Jan Gawronski. The couple moved to The Hague where her husband was given the post of First Secretary at the Polish Embassy. The day after their wedding, Pier Giorgio wrote to Marco Beltramo:

> Of course, I am happy because my sister is happy and because her husband is a good man. But at the same time, saying good-bye to her yesterday was terrible. You can imagine what it must have been like to see my only sister, my childhood friend, leaving for such a faraway place; it was a real blow to my heart.[95]

The Frassati house seemed empty without Luciana's positive presence. Alfredo and Adelaide argued constantly and Pier Giorgio now had to face that living hell alone. "In the midst of that angry silence," Luciana recalled frankly, "it was difficult to deal with the situation. Mother's irritation had reached the point that it became impossible to have any kind of relationship with her. [Pier Giorgio] was left all alone to carry the weight of the crumbling structure of our family on his shoulders . . . it was a sacrifice no day to come could possibly alleviate."[96]

Pier Giorgio really missed Luciana. "My life," he confided to Isidoro Bonini, "is going through its darkest hour of crisis, and just when my sister is going so far away."[97] Though brother and sister were very different in character—"I liked success," Luciana admitted, "while [Pier Giorgio] preferred poverty"[98]—they were bound together by a sincere and deep love. Luciana was the only one in the family in whom Pier Giorgio ever confided and from whom he sought advice. Yet, even Luciana did not know of Pier Giorgio's comings and goings among the poor and was ignorant of his work on their behalf, which explains why she sometimes found his behavior "strange." Luciana would recall with heartache:

> The sense of wanting to protect him was with me all my life. I realized his physical superiority on our mountain treks, swimming in the sea, and on our bicycle trips when he sang while I could not catch my breath. But in my awareness of his moral superiority, which others did not comprehend, I would endeavor with my lively spirit to fend off the criticism of ordinary people to his otherworldly being.[99]

Unlike Luciana, who enjoyed fashionable society and functions, Pier Giorgio avoided these like the plague. He never accompanied Luciana to dances or parties, yet the affection between them was always strong. The day Luciana left for The Hague, Pier Giorgio went to the train station to say good-bye and broke down weeping. "Unfortunately, now that we are separated by so many kilometers," he wrote to her with some sorrow a few weeks later, "now that we are apart not for just a few days, but for a lifetime and will see each other only now and

Pier Giorgio and Luciana at the Italian Embassy in Berlin (1922).

then, only now do I realize what it means to have a sister at home, and what an empty space her leaving creates."[100]

Now a period of pain, extreme renunciation, and conversion awaited Pier Giorgio. Gradually, the shadow of suffering was moving over his life.

Chapter 10

The Path to Life

In January 1925, Pier Giorgio wrote to Franz Massetti of his plans for the Holy Year decreed by Pope Pius XI. "I prepared for the Holy Year by reading Saint Augustine, which I have not finished yet, but which has given me an immense and deep joy. . . . I am also studying other writings: I am reading Papini's *Testimonianze*, after which I will turn to philosophy if I can find a good translation of Saint Thomas Aquinas. As you can see," Pier Giorgio concluded, "I've got big plans for the Holy Year."[101]

The beginning of 1925 found Pier Giorgio working hard to complete his studies for his university degree. "I am under an incredible burden of work," he told his friends.[102] Still, he was happy: "At this point, I am close to reaping what I have sown." Pier Giorgio could almost taste his future working on behalf of needy miners. He admitted to his friends, "I am really happy to be able to finish my student career in such a beautiful year."[103]

Not surprisingly, Alfredo Frassati had something entirely different in mind for Pier Giorgio's future. Unfortunately, Pier Giorgio had no idea that his father had already decided that he would become the new administrative director of *La Stampa*.

Alfredo could not have been entirely ignorant of how much Pier Giorgio's dream meant to him, but he considered it "youthful nonsense." Pier Giorgio stood to inherit a sizable amount, which, with great care, could yield even greater profit. Therefore, Alfredo deemed it necessary for his son to learn the trade, and he assigned one of his most trustworthy employees, Giuseppe Cassone, to teach the younger Frassati the ins-and-outs of the newspaper business. But Alfredo could not bring himself to deliver the news, so he asked Cassone to tell Pier Giorgio of his decision. It came as a hard blow to Pier Giorgio, who suddenly watched his dream disappearing just when he was so close to achieving the goal. With tears in his eyes, Pier Giorgio asked, "Will this please my father?" When Cassone replied in the affirmative, Pier Giorgio simply said, "Tell him I accept."

With these words, Pier Giorgio surrendered to his father's wishes and resigned himself to the situation at great personal sacrifice. This was another example of Pier Giorgio's ability to surrender what was dear to him for the good of others.

On June 20, 1925, Pier Giorgio took part in the annual procession in honor of Turin's Madonna of Consolata. There was an additional ceremony to honor the transfer of the remains of a local patron, Blessed Joseph Cafasso (canonized by Pope Pius XII in 1947), whose feast day fell on June 23. "When the urn passed in front of us," recalled one participant of the event, "there was a moment of solemn prayer, during which time I saw Pier Giorgio on his knees praying so intensely that he seemed to forget everything else around him. I must say that later, when I heard of his illness and his premature death, I came to believe that in those moments of prayer he must have offered his life to God for the salvation of those dear to him."[104] Indeed, Pier Giorgio had many reasons to pray for his family. In May, Alfredo had announced his desire to legally separate from Adelaide, and this time the rift seemed beyond repair.

Luciana returned to Turin in mid-June to find Pier Giorgio changed. He looked so much thinner and he seemed to swim in his clothes. His face looked strained, as if some painful secret was consuming him. Luciana no longer knew her brother, who had once been always happy and ready to play a practical joke. But she attributed his apparent mental and physical exhaustion to his being in the midst of a particularly intense period of final exams.

Pier Giorgio was anxious to finish school, but he often felt so lost. His university courses helped him to fight this feeling; his degree was something to focus on. "I hope to be finished in July," he told his friends, all the while fully aware that what awaited him was the career his father had chosen for him and not his own dream.

Yet, despite all of Alfredo's plans, Pier Giorgio would never become the administrative director of *La Stampa*.

On the last day of June, Pier Giorgio mentioned that he was feeling sick; he had a migraine headache and no appetite. The next morning, when he was not up as early as usual, the housemaid checked on him. The pale and thin Pier Giorgio was finding it hard to move, but he got up to study. When he could not concentrate, Pier Giorgio decided to go out for a walk. He caught up with his friend, Franz Massetti, to whom he read a few lines from the book on the life of Saint Catherine of Siena he carried with him. "How fortunate Saint Catherine was," Pier Giorgio remarked, "to have seen Jesus in this life! I envy her."

He met another friend, Ernesto Atzori, who noticed that Pier Giorgio seemed to be in pain. "I'm fine," Pier Giorgio assured him, and then added with a hint of foreboding, "if God calls me, I will gladly obey."[105] In the afternoon, Pier Giorgio accepted an invitation to go sailing down the Po River with some friends, but felt too tired. Instead, he went home exhausted, took an aspirin, and went straight to bed without eating.

At the same time, Linda Ametis, Pier Giorgio's ninety-year-old grandmother, was very ill. Diagnosed with rheumatic fever, her condition deteriorated daily. Naturally, the eyes of everyone in the Frassati household were on the sick and dying grandmother, so no one noticed Pier Giorgio's illness. When they did, everyone assumed Pier Giorgio had caught some flu, which would pass quickly. And, under the trying circumstances, the family viewed Pier Giorgio's illness as an added inconvenience.

Linda Ametis died on July 1, 1925, and still no one suspected that Pier Giorgio's strength had begun to crumble.

Though he was nearly incapable of moving, no one seemed to notice his physical condition. Weak and in pain, Pier Giorgio got up to see his grandmother for the last time. He knelt beside his grandmother's bed and prayed the Rosary. Then, with tremendous effort, Pier Giorgio struggled to stand up and walk back to his room.

It became obvious the night before Linda Ametis' funeral that Pier Giorgio would not be able to attend. Disappointed, Adelaide scolded him, "You seem to be doing this on purpose, Pier Giorgio; you are never there when you are needed."[106]

Marco Beltramo stopped by the Frassatis to visit Pier Giorgio, and they talked about what their other friends were doing and planned some mountain climbs. When Marco Beltramo expressed his deep concern at Pier Giorgio's condition, he made light of it. But it was very serious; paralysis was spreading rapidly through Pier Giorgio's body.

On July 3, a long procession followed the remains of Linda Ametis from Turin to the cemetery in Pollone. As Luciana left the house to join the funeral procession, she jokingly urged Pier Giorgio to "be better by the time we get back!" Pier Giorgio nodded with a smile.

Because of her emotional state, the family had encouraged Adelaide not to go to the burial but to stay in Turin with Pier Giorgio. When Pier Giorgio's condition visibly worsened, Adelaide called the family doctor, Luciano Alvazzi, to come to the house immediately.

During his exam, Alvazzi asked Pier Giorgio to try to get up. Pier Giorgio could not move. The doctor grasped the gravity of the situation at once and his face grew dark. His diagnosis was terrible and conclusive: poliomyelitis, an acute infectious disease that can affect the central nervous system, primarily the spinal cord, leading to rapidly progressive paralysis and death. Pier Giorgio may have contracted the virus in the home of one of the poor individuals he visited every day. As one person observed, "since there is no true giving without sacrifice, [Pier Giorgio] was dying the victim of his own good will."[107]

The Frassatis refused to accept Alvazzi's diagnosis. They consulted other doctors and sought other remedies, but it was all too late. The only serum that might have been able to save Pier Giorgio was at the Pasteur Institute in Paris, and although a family friend agreed to fly to Paris for it, a violent thunderstorm rolled in over Turin and prevented his plane from taking off.

Pier Giorgio was not afraid to die because he knew that death is "a very simple path," as he once said, "between life and Life, which must in any case never frighten us."[108] Two years earlier, in July 1923, Pier Giorgio had gone to the funeral of a fellow university student, and the event led him to reflect on the reality of death. Pier Giorgio shared his reflection in a letter to Antonio Villani.

> I reflected on the fact that a few years from now I too will be in that state; I will also wake up to compassion mixed with a sense of horror . . . in any case, this great mystery of death . . . will dissolve my body and in no time will turn it to dust. But beyond the physical body is the soul to which we must dedicate all our efforts, so that we stand before the Supreme Judge without blame, or at least little blame; this way, after a few years in purgatory, we will reach eternal peace. But how can we prepare for this great step, and when

> will it come? Since one never knows when death will come to take us away, it is wise to prepare ourselves each day as if it were our last. Therefore, from now on I am going to try to do a little something each day to prepare myself for death, so that when death finally does come I will not be caught unprepared and regret those wonderful years of youth wasted from a spiritual point of view.[109]

Pier Giorgio's physical condition continued to deteriorate, and the family called a priest. They prepared the Eucharistic table in Pier Giorgio's room according to his instructions, placing two large silver candleholders on each side of a painting of Raphael's *Madonna della Seggiola*, a gift to the Cesare Balbo Club from Pope Benedict XV that Pier Giorgio had won in a lottery three years earlier. After his confession, Pier Giorgio happily received Holy Communion.

"Giorgio, what if your grandmother calls you to join her in heaven?" the priest asked. Pier Giorgio answered without hesitation, "I would be happy," and then he added, "but what about father and mother?" The priest tried to reassure him, saying, "You will never abandon them . . . you will always be with them in spirit. You will give them your faith and your forbearance, and you will all continue to be one family." Pier Giorgio nodded his head in agreement.

Upon hearing of Pier Giorgio's condition, Cardinal Giuseppe Gamba wanted to rush to his bedside, but, as Luciana Frassati recalled, the family refused to allow anyone to disturb Pier Giorgio.[110]

Pier Giorgio's final thoughts were for "his poor." He asked his sister to bring him a box of medicines, an insurance policy, and a sheet of paper for him to write on. With an unsteady hand, Pier Giorgio wrote, "Here is Converso's medicine. The policy belongs to Sappa: I forgot about it, so renew it on my behalf." Converso and Sappa were receiving assistance from the Saint Vincent de Paul Society, and Pier Giorgio was supposed to visit them that Friday. Pier Giorgio was dying, and yet he still found the strength to put others first.

At this point Pier Giorgio could not rest because it was becoming increasingly difficult for him to breathe. During the night, he asked Sister Michelina, who kept watch at his bedside, "Please help me to make the sign of the cross." She took Pier Giorgio's hand and helped him to make this sign of faith. Around 4:00 A.M., Pier Giorgio spoke his final words: "Will you forgive me, Lord? Oh, Lord, please forgive me!"

Father Formica administered the Sacrament of the Sick. For a moment, around 10:00 A.M., Pier Giorgio emerged from sleep and looked tenderly at Luciana. Later that afternoon the polio serum arrived from Paris, but it was too late. At 7:00 P.M., on Saturday, July 4, 1925, Pier Giorgio Frassati left his fragile physical body to be clothed in light.

Luciana recalled those final moments, carved forever in her memory.

> Stunned by the enormity of what was happening, I wandered through the house, unable to rest . . . A life of barely twenty-four years, marked by such noble and secret works, and summarized by the silent agony of those six days, this young life was disappearing before our very eyes. The large clock rang seven o'clock. Mother held Pier Giorgio's head in her hands, while someone uttered a prayer. As I knelt by his bedside, with his hand and his rosary in mine, I felt one last squeeze, a final good-bye. He was gone.

He died silently with a mysterious smile on his lips. On the desk near his bed, beside his university texts, sat the Office of the Blessed Virgin Mary and the life of Saint Catherine of Siena. Just as Pier Giorgio had been born on a Saturday—a day traditionally dedicated to Mary—so he was born to heavenly life on a Saturday. He had once confided to his friends, "The day of my death will be the best day of my life."

The family laid Pier Giorgio out in his room, dressed in a dark, pinstriped suit. They placed a crucifix and a relic of Blessed Joseph Cafasso on his chest.

That very night, Clementina Luotto wrote a heart-rending letter to Marco Beltramo.

> Standing beside his bed, which seemed like an altar to me, I felt for the first time that death descended from above and he was taken up . . . Oh! The marvelous youthfulness that emanated from him, which made us all feel so lighthearted, so ready to ascend, so free from any earthly hindrances, so close to the God that was in him! Now who will give us this purifying joy? Who will renew not only for us but also in us the miracle of joyful holiness as carefree and fresh and revivifying as the water of an Alpine spring? The truth is there, on that bed, where there is an effusion of celestial peace . . . O Goodness, you are more luminous and warmer than the sun, and you are eternal![111]

On July 6, 1925, a vast crowd gathered for Pier Giorgio's funeral in the parish church of Crocetta. While the leading figures in politics, finance, and journalism gathered to pay homage to the son of Alfredo Frassati inside the church, a swarm of ordinary and anonymous people gathered outside to honor their faithful benefactor. There were workers from Turin's industrial district, the unemployed, and the homeless who lived in attics, basements, underneath the bridges spanning the Po River, or on park benches. Outside the church stood a multitude of the nameless faces, the have-nots whom Pier Giorgio had helped and loved in the name of Christ. Only then did the Frassatis begin to truly realize who Pier Giorgio really was, the son they had never understood, the strange boy they often described as good-for-nothing, "our dear big oaf, Pier Giorgio," as his mother often said. Struck with grief and remorse, the family realized they had been living with a saint—a painful but important lesson for them.

The funeral was a celebration of Pier Giorgio's life by the overflowing crowd. Eight of Pier Giorgio's fellow university students carried his casket. "Walking behind the casket," Luciana Frassati recalled, "I could not despair. I felt as if I were walking on air, taking part in a great triumph."[112]

Pier Giorgio Frassati's story left a profound impression on the public. The day after his funeral, the liberal politician, Luigi Ambrosini, wrote in *La Stampa*, "The works he performed in silence emerge from silence with his passing."[113] With great admiration, the socialist politician, Filippo Turati, wrote in the newspaper, *La Giustizia*:

> He was truly a man, this Pier Giorgio Frassati. . . . The things we read about him are so new and extraordinary that it fills with reverent wonder even those who do not share his faith. He believed in God, professed his faith with open worship, conceiving it as a form of soldiering, like a uniform one puts on before the world without ever changing it into something ordinary for the sake of accommodation or opportun-

> ism or human respect. . . . This young Catholic man was foremost a Christian who translated his mystical beliefs into concrete acts of human kindness. This young engineering student with the serene and sweet eyes of a man who feels everyone is his brother, especially the most miserable and unhappy, was an exceptional person we should stop to take note of . . . This Christian who believed and acted according to his beliefs, who spoke what he felt and did as he said, this uncompromising defender of his faith is a model who has something to teach us all.[114]

In the Gospel of John, we read that the grain of wheat must die if it is to bear fruit (cf. 12:24). After Pier Giorgio's death, Alfredo and Adelaide Frassati resolved to make their marriage work. Alfredo returned to the practice of his faith and always attributed this grace to Pier Giorgio, and, in 1961, Alfredo died at the age of ninety-three after receiving the sacraments.

Once, Alfredo expressed remorse tinged with nostalgia as he spoke to his sister-in-law, Elena, about Pier Giorgio.

> No one understood what Giorgio meant to me: he was my pride, my passion; I saw in him all the things I wished I could be, but I also saw myself in his stubborn and kind character. I saw my affection in his love for the poor, and it seemed to me that the little bit of good there is in me was multiplied by the millions in Pier Giorgio.[115]

The artist Alberto Falchetti painted a portrait of Pier Giorgio that captured the beauty and spirit of that remarkable youth: his dark hair, his regular features, the slight smile on his face, and his penetrating glance. Reproduced many times, the portrait adorns the walls of hundreds of youth offices of Catholic Action all over Italy and organizations under his patronage. This portrait has attracted the attention of countless numbers of young people who have come to know Pier Giorgio through this portrait.

Thérèse of Lisieux said prophetically that she would spend her heaven doing good on earth, which would be "like a shower of roses." It seems providential that Pier Giorgio Frassati was born to eternal life only a few months after the Church solemnly proclaimed a saint that "humble flower transplanted to Mount Carmel." And, like Saint Thérèse, Pier Giorgio's death heralded his hour of victory.

Chapter 11

A Saint for Our Times

Pier Giorgio's life, wrapped in an aura of holiness, attracted the devotion of a growing number of people soon after his death, and the process for his beatification was initiated. The process for canonization is a long and complex one, and the pronouncement of Pier Giorgio's candidacy for sainthood was a considerable undertaking that lasted over fifty years and required the examination of a mountain of documents.

The first ecclesiastical step toward beatification, the *Informativo ordinario*, began on July 2, 1932, at the behest of Turin's archbishop, Cardinal Maurilio Fossati. Twenty-five first-hand testimonials were heard between July and October 1935. Two Salesian fathers led this first stage of the process. On December 21, 1938, the Vatican issued the decree of *nulla osta*, declaring that nothing stood in the way of proceeding with Pier Giorgio's beatification.

Despite this decree, in December 1941 anonymous sources called Pier Giorgio's moral integrity into question. These sources raised concerns regarding Pier Giorgio's relationship with Laura Hidalgo and a camping trip Pier Giorgio and his friends had made when he was fourteen years old. Pope Pius XII decided to proceed with caution and placed the process of beatification on hold. Perhaps the delay was providential, for the time was not yet ripe for Pier Giorgio: in many ways, he was too modern, too far ahead of many of his contemporaries.

However, Luciana refused to be passive, and between the years 1949 and 1951, she gathered an impressive number of testimonials, declarations, and other documents concerning her brother's life. Twenty-five files of documentation were sent to the office of the Under-Secretary of State for the Holy See, Monsignor Giovanni Battista Montini, the future Pope Paul VI. Montini handed the exhaustive documentation over to the Franciscan friar Gaetano Stano, who, in 1953, declared the possibility of reopening the cause of Pier Giorgio.

In 1965, Montini, now Pope Paul VI, appointed the Jesuit priest Paolo Molinari to head a careful examination of various aspects of Frassati's life. Two years later, Molinari handed the pope a sixty-five-page report, which formally reopened the cause for beatification. On June 12, 1978, a visibly pleased Paul VI officially signed the introduction to the cause for the beatification of Pier Giorgio Frassati.

On July 16, 1980, the apostolic process began under the guidance of the Archbishop of Turin, Cardinal Anastasio Ballestrero. There were seventy sessions held to hear some twenty-eight testimonies, as well as an "identification" of Pier Giorgio's mortal remains on March 31, 1981. Those present for the exhumation, as well as photos taken that day, witness that Pier Giorgio's remains were completely incorrupt—his face still had a slight smile and his supple hands held his precious rosary.

July 29, 1981 marked the formal closing of the apostolic process and the Acts were sent to the Congregation for the Causes of Saints in Rome. From then on, Pier Giorgio's journey to the altar of the saints moved swiftly. On June 12, 1987, the *Positio super virtutibus* was formally presented, and, on October 23 of that same year, Pope John Paul II declared Pier Giorgio "Venerable."

For an individual's beatification, it is necessary to prove that a miracle—certified to have occurred without scientific explanation—has occurred through that person's intercession, as well as a consistent indication of graces received in that person's name (*fama signorum*). In Pier Giorgio's case, miracles and graces numbered in the thousands.

Among the many miracles attributed to the intercession of Pier Giorgio, the one chosen by the Church for his beatification involved a man named Domenico Sellan. Born in 1892 at San Quirino di Pordenone, Sellan suffered from a serious form of tuberculosis. Wounded in the spine during the First World War, Sellan was paralyzed and bed-ridden, and, nearing his death, he was a man without faith. On December 28, 1933, the local parish priest gave him a small holy card of Pier Giorgio Frassati so that Sellan could pray the prayer. After a few hours, Sellan called for the priest and asked him to hear his confession, after which Sellan received the Eucharist. Instead of dying as everyone expected, Sellan lived for another thirty-five years!

The canonical process for Pier Giorgio's beatification closed in Turin on January 31, 1989. The Acts of this stage of the process were sent to the Vatican where the documentation, which included the account of Sellan's miracle, received the approval of the medical board of the Congregation for the Causes of Saints, the special Congress of Theologians, and the Congregation of Cardinals. On December 21 of that same year, Pope John Paul II officially declared Sellan's case a miracle attributed to Pier Giorgio's intercession. The way was now clear for Pier Giorgio's elevation to the altar of the saints.

On Sunday, May 20, 1990, over fifty thousand faithful gathered in Saint Peter's Square to celebrate the beatification of Pier Giorgio Frassati. The "man of the Eight Beatitudes," as John Paul II called him, was now "Blessed Frassati"—one step away from sainthood.

When Pier Giorgio's picture was draped across the central balcony of Saint Peter's Basilica, the crowd roared in an explosion of joy. Pier Giorgio's feast day was established as July 4, the day he left this earthly existence for eternal life in heaven.

In his homily for the beatification, John Paul II observed:

> At first glance, Pier Giorgio Frassati's style, as a modern young man full of life, seems rather ordinary. Yet this is precisely the originality of his virtue, which invites us to reflect on his life and which encourages us to imitate him. In him, faith and everyday life went hand in hand, so that faithfulness to the Gospel translated into a loving concern for the poor and the needy, which continued until the very last days of the illness that claimed his life. His taste for beauty and for art, his passion for sport and for the mountains, his concern for the problems of society never stood in the way of his constant relationship with the Absolute.

People from all over the world gathered at St. Peter's Square on May 20, 1990, as Pope John Paul II beatified Pier Giorgio Frassati.

> Everything was immersed in the mystery of God and everything was devoted to serving others: this is how we can summarize his earthly day![116]

On September 16, 1990, Pier Giorgio's mortal remains were transferred from the cemetery in Pollone and placed beneath a side altar in Turin's Cathedral of Saint John the Baptist. Now the site of a stream of pilgrims, people come to pray for the day when the Church finally declares Pier Giorgio a saint.

Many favors and miracles are attributed to his intercession, and the testimonies collected tell of many heavenly "favors" received through the prayers of Pier Giorgio Frassati: families on the verge of breaking up were reunited, serious economic problems were resolved, reconciliations occurred between former enemies, religious vocations were discerned or saved, physical healings that science cannot explain happened, and exceptional spiritual graces were obtained with Pier Giorgio's loving, "helping hand."

In the Gospel, Jesus tells us that one can know a tree by its fruits, and the fruits borne by Pier Giorgio Frassati are truly amazing. There are some 1,500 groups in the world named after Frassati and many schools, oratories, chapels, sports centers, student clubs, and university groups claim him as their patron. His image is everywhere: in catechism classes, at conferences, in books, in periodicals, in scholarly studies.

The world celebrated the one-hundredth anniversary of Pier Giorgio's birth with numerous initiatives and special ceremonies. On April 6, 2001, the Polytechnic University of Turin conferred a degree in mining engineering to the memory of Blessed Pier Giorgio Frassati. Countless numbers of people celebrated Pier Giorgio's birthday via the Internet.

Pier Giorgio, the "frightful mountain climber" as his father sometimes called him, has also inspired many mountain climbing groups all over the world. Truly, Pier Giorgio's life is a landscape of holiness that radiates around the world, representing a source of grace and richness for the whole Church and for the entire family of the baptized.

In his apostolic exhortation, *Christifideles Laici* (Lay Members of Christ's Faithful People), Pope John Paul II wrote:

> How can one not notice the ever-growing existence of *religious indifference* and *atheism* in its more varied forms, particularly in its perhaps most widespread form of *secularism*? Adversely affected by the impressive triumphs of continuing scientific and technological development and above all, fascinated by a very old and yet new temptation, namely, that of wishing to become like God (cf. Gen 3:5) through the use of a liberty without bounds, individuals cut the religious roots that are in their hearts; they forget God, or simply retain him without meaning in their lives, or outrightly reject him, and begin to adore various "idols" of the contemporary world (no. 3).

And yet, as the Holy Father reminds us:

> *Human longing and the need for religion*, however, are not able to be totally extinguished. When persons in conscience have the courage to face the more serious questions of human existence—particularly questions related to the purpose of life, to suffering and to dying—they are unable to avoid making their own the words of truth uttered by Saint Augustine: "You have made us for yourself, O Lord, and our hearts are restless until they rest in you." In the

> same manner the present-day world bears witness to this as well, in ever-increasing and impressive ways, through an openness to a spiritual and transcendent outlook towards life, the renewed interest in religious research, the return to a sense of the sacred and to prayer, and the demand for freedom to call upon the name of the Lord (no. 4).
>
> To all people of today I once again repeat the impassioned cry with which I began my pastoral ministry: "*Do not be afraid! Open, indeed, open wide the doors to Christ!* Open to his saving power the confines of states, and systems political and economic, as well as the vast fields of culture, civilization, and development. Do not be afraid! Christ knows 'what is inside a person.' Only he knows! Today too often people do not know what they carry inside, in the deepest recesses of their soul, in their heart. Too often people are uncertain about a sense of life on earth. Invaded by doubts they are led into despair. Therefore—with humility and trust I beg and implore you—allow Christ to speak to the person in you. Only he has the words of life, yes, eternal life (no. 34).

Throughout his brief life, Pier Giorgio always opened his heart to Christ and allowed the Spirit of God to transform him. As a model for young believers, Pier Giorgio's life is a challenge to today's world, caught between secularization and cultural emptiness. As the priest-journalist, Father Primo Soldi, aptly put it, "Pier Giorgio challenges the 'instinctual humanism' that seems so popular among young people today. In the face of this kind of humanism, that sees value in doing whatever 'feels good,' Frassati offers the model of someone who realizes his full potential by being true to himself."

Pier Giorgio's story speaks to young people today, just as his example influenced his contemporaries. When Pope John Paul II visited Pier Giorgio's tomb in July 1989, the Holy Father said, "I also felt the positive influence of Pier Giorgio's example and, as a student, I was always impressed by the strength of his Christian witness."[117]

With Pier Giorgio Frassati, holiness comes down from the pedestal on which we have placed it and speaks to us in everyday language. His is a holiness that is planted firmly on the ground and walks a path everyone can follow. This witness of simple Christian joy inspires and calls out to us. It shows us that sanctity is only possible if we listen to the Gospel and put into practice its central message: love one another. In the words of the theologian Karl Rahner:

> Frassati is a Christian, simply, and in an absolutely spontaneous way, as if it were something spontaneous for everyone. He had the strength and the courage to be what he was . . . from [the perspective of] Christian reality itself: that God is what sustains us is prayer, that the Eucharist nourishes what is eternal in us, that all people are brothers. Love for the poor, responsibility in facing the wretchedness of others were (or became?) so genuine and deep, so charged with the spirit of sacrifice in Pier Giorgio as to make him an exception among the many Christian young people of the time.[118]

Pier Giorgio did nothing extraordinary or dramatic during his life. He did not found a religious order; he was not a missionary to faraway lands; he did not preach to crowds. Rather, quite simply, he staked everything on God with the absolute certainty that, as he once wrote, "By yourself you can accomplish nothing, but if you place God at the center of all your actions, then you will reach the ultimate goal."[119]

Appendix A

From the Letters of Pier Giorgio Frassati

In a world gone astray from God there is no peace, but it also lacks charity, which is true and perfect love. . . . Nothing is more beautiful than love. Indeed, faith and hope will end when we die, whereas love, that is, charity, will last for eternity; if anything, I think it will be even more alive in the next life.

We who, by the grace of God, are Catholics, must not squander the best years of our lives as so many unhappy young people do, who worry about enjoying the good things in life, things that do not in fact bring any good, but rather the fruit of immorality in today's world. We must prepare ourselves to be ready and able to handle the struggles we will have to endure to fulfill our goals, and, in so doing, to give our country happier and morally healthier days in the near future. But in order for this to happen we need the following: constant prayer to obtain God's grace, without which all our efforts are in vain; organization and discipline to be ready for action at the right moment; and finally, we need to sacrifice our own passions, indeed our very selves, because without this sacrifice we will never achieve our goal.

By drawing closer to the poor, little by little we become their confidants and counselors in the worst moments of this earthly pilgrimage. We can give them the comforting words of faith and often we succeed, not by our own merit, in putting on the right road people who have strayed without meaning to.

Witnessing daily the faith with which some families often bear the worst suffering, their constant sacrifices, and that they do all this for the love of God, often makes us ask why we, who have received so many things from God, have been so neglectful, so bad, while they, who have not been as privileged, are so much better? And so we resolve in our conscience to follow the way of the cross, the only way that leads to eternal life.

May peace reign in your soul . . . any other gift we possess in this life is vanity, just as all the things of this world are vain.

With every day that passes, I grow more and more convinced of how ugly the world is, of how much suffering there is, and, unfortunately, of how it is the good who suffer the most. Meanwhile, we who have been given so many of God's blessings have repaid him poorly. This is an awful reality that racks my brain; while I'm studying, every so often I ask myself: will I continue on the right path? Will I have the strength to persevere all the way? In the face of this pang of doubt, the faith given to me in Baptism reassures me of this: by yourself, you will accomplish nothing, but if you place God at the center of all your actions, then you will reach the goal.

In God's marvelous plan, Divine Providence often uses the tiniest twigs to do good works. . . . What would life be without acts of charity?

Each of you knows that the foundation of our faith is charity. Without it, our religion would crumble. We will never be truly Catholic unless we conform our entire lives to the two commandments that are the essence of the Catholic faith: to love the Lord, our God, with all our strength, and to love our neighbor as ourselves. . . . With charity, we sow the seeds of that true peace which only our faith in Jesus Christ can give us by making us all brothers and sisters. I know that this way is steep, and difficult, and strewn with thorns, while at first glance the other path seems easier, more pleasant, and more satisfying. But the fact is, if we could look into the hearts of those who follow the perverse paths of this world, we would see that they lack the serenity that comes to those who have faced a thousand difficulties and who have renounced material pleasure to follow God's law.

We are living through difficult days because the persecution against the Church is raging more than ever, but this should not frighten you, brave and good young people. Always remember that the Church is a divine institution and it cannot come to an end.

Foolish is he who follows the pleasures of this world, because these are always fleeting and bring much pain. The only true pleasure is that which comes to us through faith.

Come, and your every sacrifice will be repaid in heaven, because Jesus Christ promises that everything we do for the poor in his name we do for him. You do not want to deny Christ this love, He whose infinite love for humanity gave himself to us in the sacrament of Eucharist, as our Comforter and the Bread of Life.

I hope that by the grace of God I will continue to follow these Catholic ideals so that one day, in the way God wishes, I will be able to preserve and promote these truths.

It is a difficult battle, but we must strive to win it and to rediscover our small road to Damascus in order to walk toward the destination to which we all must arrive. . . . What is clear is that faith is the only anchor of salvation and we must hold tightly to it: without it, what would our lives be? Nothing, or rather, wasted, because in life there is only suffering, and suffering without faith is unbearable. But suffering that is nourished by the flame of faith becomes something beautiful, because it tempers the soul to deal with suffering.

In order to be Christian, our lives must be a continual renunciation and sacrifice. However, we know that the difficulties of this world are nothing compared to the eternal happiness that awaits us, where there will be no limit to our joy, no end to our happiness, and we shall enjoy unimaginable peace. And so, young people, learn from our Lord Jesus Christ the meaning of sacrifice.

When you are totally consumed by the Eucharistic fire, then you will be able more consciously to thank God, who has called you to become part of his family. Then you will enjoy the peace that those who are happy in this world have never experienced, because true happiness, oh young people, does not consist in the pleasures of this world, or in earthly things, but in peace of conscience, which we only have if we are pure of heart and mind.

A Catholic cannot help but be happy; sadness should be banished from their souls. Suffering is not sadness, which is the worst disease. This disease is almost always caused by atheism, but the end for which we are created guides us along life's pathway, which may be strewn with thorns, but is not sad. It is happy even through suffering.

Appendix B

Pier Giorgio Frassati's Life Touches the World: What Others Have Said

"Sanctify Christ as Lord in your hearts. Always be ready to give an explanation to anyone who asks you for a reason for your hope" (1 Pt 3:15).

In our century, Pier Giorgio Frassati incarnated these words of Saint Peter in his own life. The power of the Spirit of Truth, united to Christ, made him a modern witness to the hope which springs from the Gospel and to the grace of salvation which works in human hearts. Thus, he became a living witness and courageous defender of this hope in the name of Christian youth of the twentieth century.

Faith and charity, the true driving forces of his existence, made him active and diligent in the milieu in which he lived, in his family and school, in the university and society; they transformed him into a joyful, enthusiastic apostle of Christ, a passionate follower of his message and charity.

The secret of his apostolic zeal and holiness is to be sought in the ascetical and spiritual journey which he traveled: in prayer and in persevering adoration, even at night, of the Blessed Sacrament; in his thirst for the Word of God, which he sought in biblical texts; in the peaceful acceptance of life's difficulties, in family life as well; in chastity lived as a cheerful, uncompromising discipline; in his daily love of silence and life's "ordinariness."

It is precisely in these factors that we are given to understand the deep wellspring of his spiritual vitality. Indeed, it is through the Eucharist that Christ communicates his Spirit; it is through listening to the word that the readiness to welcome others grows, and it is also through prayerful abandonment to God's will that life's great decisions mature. Only by adoring God who is present in his or her own heart can the baptized Christian respond to the person who "asks you for a reason for your hope" (1 Pt 3:15). And the young Frassati knew it, felt it, lived it. In his life, faith was fused with charity: firm in faith and active in charity, because without works, faith is dead (cf. Jas 2:20).

Certainly, at a superficial glance, Frassati's lifestyle, that of a modern young man who was full of life, does not present anything out of the ordinary. This, however, is the originality of his virtue, which invites us to reflect upon it and impels us to imitate it. In him faith and daily events are harmoniously fused, so that adherence to the Gospel is translated into loving care for the poor and the needy in a continual crescendo until the very last days of the sickness which led to his death. His love for beauty and art, his passion for sports and mountains, his attention to society's problems did not inhibit his constant relationship with the Absolute.

Entirely immersed in the mystery of God and totally dedicated to the constant service of his neighbor—thus we can sum up his earthly life! He fulfilled his vocation as a lay Christian in many associative and political involvements in a society in ferment, a society which was indifferent and sometimes even hostile to the Church. In this spirit, Pier Giorgio succeeded in giving new impulse to various Catholic movements, which he enthusiastically joined, but especially to Catholic Action, as well as the Federation of Italian Catholic University Students [FUCI], in which he found the true gymnasium of his Christian training and the right fields of his apostolate. In Catholic Action he joyfully and proudly lived his Christian vocation and strove to love Jesus and to see in him the brothers and sisters whom he met on his way or whom he actively sought in their places of suffering, marginalization, and isolation in order to help them feel the warmth of his human solidarity and the supernatural comfort of faith in Christ.

He died young, at the end of a short life, but one which was extraordinarily filled with spiritual fruits, setting out for his "true homeland and singing God's praises."

By his example he proclaims that a life lived in Christ's Spirit, the Spirit of the Beatitudes, is "blessed," and that only the person who becomes a "man or woman of the Beatitudes" can succeed in communicating love and peace to others. He repeats that it is really worth giving up everything to serve the Lord. He testifies that holiness is possible for everyone, and that only the revolution of charity can enkindle the hope of a better future in the hearts of people.

Indeed, [Pier Giorgio's] entire life seems to sum up Christ's words which we find in John's Gospel: "Whoever loves me will keep my word, and my Father will love him, and we will come and make our dwelling with him" (Jn 14:23).

This is the "inner" person loved by the Father, loved because he or she has loved much! Is not love what is most needed in our century, at its beginning, as well as at its end? Is it perhaps not true that the only thing that lasts, without ever losing its validity, is the fact that a person "has loved"?

He left this world rather young, but he made a mark upon our entire century, and not only on our century. He left this world, but in the Easter power of his Baptism, he can say to everyone, especially to the young generations of today and tomorrow: "You will see me, because I live and you will live" (Jn 14:19).

These words were spoken by Jesus Christ when he took leave of his Apostles before undergoing his Passion. I like to think of them as forming on the lips of our new Blessed himself as a persuasive invitation to live from Christ and in Christ. This invitation is still valid, it is valid today as well, especially for today's young people, valid for everyone. It is a valid invitation which Pier Giorgio Frassati has left for us. Amen.

Pope John Paul II
Homily at the Beatification of Pier Giorgio Frassati

Pier Giorgio is a Christian who becomes a fellow traveler of the marginalized, and, in so doing, he offers them, and himself, a witness to the Gospel. . . . His amazing witness as a believer expressed itself in everyday life, to the very best of his Christian and human potential. It was a witness lived in ordinary ways, but on the frontier of the Kingdom, as a radical choice to live in the imitation of Christ. . . . Senator Frassati's son was a young man who, in ordinary ways, gave extraordinary witness to the Christian ideals of his generation. A man of God and a man of his own times.

Alberto Monticone
Historian

As a young man fascinated by Pier Giorgio's passion for sports, I desperately dreamed of joining one of his hikes. This conqueror of mountain peaks, this life of the party, this consoler of the poor, this militant of social action was first and foremost a mystic. His overflowing energy and youthful exuberance drew strength from an intimate union with the living Christ, whom he breathed in like the fresh air from those mountain peaks.

Cardinal Roger Etchegaray

We knew he was a studious boy, pious and respectful. The good priests never ceased to hold him up to us as a model.

Of course, those friends who are considered good, studious, religious, and the kind of students your teachers praise as models for others are always hated. So you can only imagine what we thought of Pier Giorgio! And yet, with Pier Giorgio, it was different. Even though the good priests did all they could to make us hate him, we all liked Pier Giorgio, always.

Mario Soldati
Author and director

I recall the impression that Frassati made on me . . . I have to confess frankly that I thought of him as just one among many Christian young people in the Catholic youth movement of the time—there were so many. This impression should be understood as praise not disparagement. Frassati represented the pure, happy, handsome Christian youth, devoted to prayer, enthusiastic about everything that is free and beautiful, interested in social problems, who had the Church and its future at heart, and a serene and manly spontaneity. . . . Here we have someone who lived his Christianity with a naturalness that is almost awe-inspiring, surprisingly unproblematic and inviting. In fact, his problems, often bathed in silent tears, were immersed in the grace of his faith: in prayer, Holy Communion, and in loving his neighbor.

Karl Rahner, S.J.
Theologian

I recognized in [Pier Giorgio] the young Christian to whom we can look to as a model, someone who knew what it means to make of his life an offering to God and to others, all through fidelity to the way of life: prayer, Eucharist, the Word of God, sacrifice, and dedication to others.

Giuseppe Lazzati
Professor and rector, Catholic University of Milan

That limitless generosity with which he gave to others, in which he truly gave all of himself, was the fruit of a process of deep inner growth, which he achieved rather quickly in life. Pier Giorgio understood that the individual truly realizes his potential and sanctifies himself only to the extent that he is willing to give.

Carla Casalengo
Author

A saint, a friend for all of us, but especially for those who today encounter the novelty of the Christian message, Pier Giorgio Frassati's witness is an enthusiastic confirmation of the reasonableness and the humanity of Christianity. It is a "provocation" to which the heart—especially that of the young—can open itself. Pier Giorgio challenges the "instinctual humanism" that seems so popular among young people today. In the face of this kind of humanism, that sees value in doing whatever "feels good," Frassati offers the model of someone who realizes his full potential by being true to himself.

Father Primo Soldi
Priest and journalist

As far as I know, Pier Giorgio never worked a miracle during his lifetime. He never founded a religious order or started a new reform movement. But he had his priorities straight. He said, "In this trying time that our country is going through, we Catholics and especially we students have a serious duty to fulfill: our self-formation." These words ring true for laypeople in this country today. God calls each of us who have been baptized to a continual preparation to serve him so that when he gives us the opportunity we are ready. Pier Giorgio lived his life on this model. He simply set Jesus Christ as his first priority, and sought him in every situation, in every person, in every task set before him. And it was there, in the everyday business of life, that he found his God and the fullness of life.

Brother R. F. King, O.P.

Appendix C

Living the Gospel in Politics and Charity

In 1927, in an address to university students, Pope Pius XI said: "The political field is a field for a wider form of charity: political charity." These words seem to summarize Pier Giorgio Frassati's understanding of politics as a form of service.

In 1920, at age nineteen, Pier Giorgio joined the Italian Popular Party or Catholic Party begun by Father Luigi Sturzo, and devoted all of his energies to the organization. Pier Giorgio got involved and was not afraid of getting his hands dirty, so to speak, or of doing his share for the common good. Pier Giorgio's political involvement and social concern were two aspects of a single ideal: serving the Kingdom of God.

Often the world of politics seems diametrically opposed to the world of faith, and faith seems to be a private matter that should never enter the public realm. However, the Church teaches that "Serving humankind and society in general with the strength of love, in the light of the Gospel and the doctrine of the Church, Christians demonstrate that Christ the Savior is present in history and gives us the gift of salvation."[120] The Second Vatican Council's document, *Gaudium et Spes*, also defined political action as a particular form of charity, and, more recently, in his Apostolic Exhortation, *Christifideles Laici*, John Paul II reaffirmed this understanding of political action:

> In order to achieve their task directed to the Christian animation of the temporal order, in the sense of serving persons and society, the lay faithful *are never to relinquish their participation in "public life,"* that is, in the many different economic, social, legislative, administrative and cultural areas, which are intended to promote organically and institutionally the *common good*. The Synod Fathers have repeatedly affirmed that every person has a right and duty to participate in public life, albeit in a diversity and complementarity of forms, levels, tasks and responsibilities. Charges of careerism, idolatry of power, egoism and corruption that are oftentimes directed at persons in government, parliaments, the ruling classes, or political parties, as well as the common opinion that participating in politics is an absolute moral danger, does not in the least justify either skepticism or an absence on the part of Christians in public life (no. 42).

Therefore, it is a right and duty of every sincere Christian to transform society in light of the Gospel value of justice. Sin leads to disorder; when multiplied many times over sin leads to socially structured sinfulness that wears away at the fundamental fabric of civil society, and erodes the humanity and spirit of a nation and its people. For this reason, the social doctrine of the Church intervenes in the life of the faithful and, by reading the history of humanity in the light of the Gospels, calls believers to their unique vocation of witnessing to Christ in the world and teaches the need for justice and peace according to God's plan.

The Church's particular interest in social questions over the past several decades has evolved through the teachings of the popes, beginning with Pope Leo XIII's 1891 encyclical, *Rerum Novarum*. In it, Leo XIII affirmed the principle of the State governed by the rule of law, that is, the development of a legal concept of the State to preserve and promote the common good. The person always comes before the State, a personalized concept of society forcefully affirmed by the teachings of Pope John XXIII (see, for example, his encyclical *Pacem in Terris*, 1963).

The development of peoples, the inalienable dignity of the human person, and the devotion of Christians toward others are all outlined in *Gaudiem et Spes* (1965), as well as in Paul VI's encyclical, *Populorum Progressio* (1967). These ideas find their greatest expression in the teaching of John Paul II (see *Centesimus Annus* and *Sollicitudo Rei Socialis*), which identifies political action as the fulfillment of the Gospel command to love one another in the service of the common good.

Roughly a century ago, Saint Pier Giorgio Frassati was inspired by this commandment of love: to serve God by serving others. This is the unique vocation of the lay person in the world. There is the temptation to excuse ourselves from action by claiming Pier Giorgio lived in an age when Christians could be more easily involved in politics. However true this may be, we are no less responsible now than Pier Giorgio was then.

As a man whose faith was deeply engaged in the world, Pier Giorgio Frassati generously devoted himself to the ecclesial and civil life of his age. He was a Christian profoundly committed to promoting justice and truth, and he shows us that the human vocation is both earthly and heavenly. With a truly democratic spirit, far ahead of his times, Pier Giorgio Frassati gave two distinct forms of Christian commitment: political action and good works.

Without running away from the world or alienating ourselves from our historic reality, we can imitate Pier Giorgio's ability to join politics with charity. Politics is integral to the development of the person and must become for us an act of love and service toward others.

As Pope John Paul II reminds us:

> Above all, it is indispensable that they have a more exact knowledge—and this demands a more widespread and precise presentation—of the *Church's social doctrine,* as repeatedly stressed by the Synod Fathers in their presentations. They refer to the participation of the lay faithful in public life, in the following words: "But for the lay faithful to take up actively this noble purpose in political matters, it is not enough to exhort them. They must be offered a proper formation of a social conscience, especially in the Church's social teaching, which contains principles of reflection, criteria for judging and practical directives (cf. Congregation for the Doctrine of the Faith, *Instruction on Christian Freedom and Liberation*, no. 72), and which must be present

in general catechetical instruction and in specialized gatherings, as well as in schools and universities. Nevertheless, this social doctrine of the Church is dynamic; that is, adapted to circumstances of time and place. It is the right and duty of Pastors to propose moral principles even concerning the social order and of all Christians to apply them in defense of human rights. Nevertheless, active participation in political parties is reserved to the lay faithful (*Christifideles Laici*, no. 60).

Appendix D

Pier Giorgio Frassati on the Internet

In our age when many people surf the Internet in search of the sacred, there is no doubt that sites exist to satisfy this hunger. Even the Vatican, dioceses, parishes, lay organizations, religious orders, cloistered convents, and individual priests and religious have web sites and email addresses.

Rapid communication is a unique dimension of modern society, yet the means of communication can be a rather fragile and often contradictory and ambiguous medium. Nevertheless, it also offers limitless possibilities for the Church's apostolic mission in the twenty-first century.

In his message on the World Day of Social Communication 2002, Pope John Paul II spoke of new frontiers of evangelization, calling the Internet the "new pulpit" from which to proclaim the Gospel at the beginning of Christianity's third millennium. This great communicator urges us neither to fear the new means of communication nor to demonize them. The

Internet is a crossroads where the good and bad meet; it presents many dangers, but many opportunities as well, which the Catholic Church can use for the new evangelization.

A list of web addresses for sites on Saint Pier Giorgio Frassati follows. One important site belongs to the Pier Giorgio Frassati International Association (piergiorgiofrassati.org), a group, based in Rome, which acts as a hub for the initiatives springing up in Pier Giorgio's name all over the world.

- www.piergiorgiofrassati.org
- www.frassatiusa.org

Notes

Introduction

1. Saint Thérèse of the Child Jesus, *Story of a Soul*, trans. John Clarke, O.C.D. (Washington: ICS Publications, 1976), 267.

2. C. Casalegno, *Pier Giorgio Frassati* (Piemme: Casale Mon-ferrato [AL], 1993), 8–9.

Chapter 1

3. Alfredo Frassati, *La Stampa-Gazzetta Piemontese*, February 7/8, 1895; V. Castronovo, *La Stampa*, 1867–1925: Un'idea di democrazia liberale, (Milan: Franco Angeli, 1988); Luciana Frassati, Un uomo, un giornale (Rome: Ed. di Storia e Letteratura, 1978).

4. Alfredo Frassati spent some time as a student in Germany and became fluent in German, which later facilitated his appointment as ambassador to Germany.

5. Luciana Frassati, *Pier Giorgio Frassati: I giorni della sua vita* (Rome: Edizioni Studium, 1975), 34.

6. Pier Giorgio Frassati, *Lettere* (1906–1925) (Milan: Vita e Pensiero, 1995), 3.

7. A. Cojazzi, *Pier Giorgio Frassati* (Turin: SEI, 1990), 31.

8. L. Frassati, *Pier Giorgio Frassati: I giorni*, 39.

Chapter 2

9. P. G. *Frassati, Lettere*, 13.

10. Gabriele D'Annuncio was an Italian poet, novelist, dramatist, and soldier. He was living in France when the First World War began. Upon returning to Italy, he spoke in support of the country joining the Allied Powers and was influential in persuading Italy to join the war.

11. Congregation for the Causes of Saints, *Canonizationis Servi Dei Petri Georgii Frassati: Positio super virtutibus* (Rome: Tipografia Guerra, 1987), vol. I, 189.

12. P. G. Frassati, *Lettere*, 83.

Chapter 3

13. L. Frassati, *Pier Giorgio Frassati: I giorni*, 89.

14. Ibid., 91.

15. Ibid., 87.

16. P. G. Frassati, *Lettere*, 34.

17. The Treaty of Versailles, signed on June 28, 1919, required that Germany make hefty payments to the victorious powers. Many at the time, and many historians since, have argued that the terms of the treaty were unfair and punitive, and created such economic weakness and political instability in Germany that it was vulnerable to the rise of Adolf Hitler and the Nazi Party.

18. L. Frassati, *Pier Giorgio Frassati: I giorni*, 64.

19. P. G. Frassati, *Lettere*, 140.

20. Ibid., 164.

21. Ibid., 138.

22. Ibid., 156.

23. Ibid., 138.

24. A political movement with origins in the First World War, Fascism became an official political party in 1921, under the leadership of Benito Mussolini. The party, with its name originating in an invented word, *fascismo*, was a movement that attempt to provide a political alternative to the two dominant political ideologies and systems of government of the day: liberal parliamentary democracy on the one hand, and socialism on the other. Mussolini's Fascists would use violence and intimidation, even murder, to silence their opponents. This explains Pier Giorgio's pessimism.

25. Benito Mussolini, the founder and leader of the Italian Fascist Party, became Prime Minister in 1922, after his Fascists used violence and intimidation to win votes and gain seats in the Italian parliament.

26. P. G. Frassati, *Lettere*, 173.

27. Dante Alighieri, *The Divine Comedy: Purgatorio*, canto VI, trans. Charles S. Singleton (Princeton: Princeton University Press, 1973), 59.

28. P. G. Frassati, *Lettere*, 136.

29. B. Gariglio, "Pier Giorgio e il fascismo," in *Il nostro tempo*, June 10, 2001.

30. Cf. Luciana Frassati, *L'impegno sociale e politico di Pier Giorgio* (Rome: Editrice AVE, 1978), 88.

Chapter 4

31. The *Non expedit* reflected the Holy See's reaction to the way in which Italy was unified in the nineteenth century, and, in particular, the military assault on Rome in 1870 that culminated in the loss of the pope's control over the city and surrounding area. The Church responded by refusing to recognize the legitimacy of the new Italian State—something that would not happen "officially" until after the First World War.

32. The Italian Popular Party, sometimes referred to as the "Catholic Party," was established in 1919 by Father Luigi Sturzo to represent the interests of Italian Catholics and promote the social teachings of the Church in politics and society.

33. See G. Candeloro, *Il movimento cattolico in Italia* (Rome: Editori Riuniti, 1974); *Cristiani in politica: I programmi politici dei movimenti cattolici democratici* (Milan: Franco Angeli, 1979). See also *Luigi Sturzo e la tradizione cattolico-popolare* (Brescia: Morcelliana, 1984); P. Spriano, *Socialismo e classe operaia a Torino dal 1892 al 1913* (Turin: Einaudi, 1958); *I cattolici in Piemonte: Lineamenti storici* (Turin: Quaderno del Centro Studi Carlo Trabucco, 1982).

34. P. G. Frassati, *Lettere*, 135.

35. Ibid., 162–163.

36. Ibid., 151.

37. F. Antonioli, et al., *Pier Giorgio Frassati*, 24.

38. See Castronovo, *La Stampa*. See also, *Giornalismo e cultura cattolica a Torino* (Turin: Quaderni del Centro Studi Carlo Trabucco, 1982); N. Tranfaglia, *La stampa quotidiana e l'avvento del regime 1922–1925* (Bari: Laterza, 1980).

39. P. G. Frassati, *Lettere*, 129–130.

40. Ibid., 145.

41. Ibid., 269.

42. F. Antonioli, et al., *Pier Giorgio Frassati*, 83.

43. G. L. Furfaro, "Il mio Pier Giorgio," in *Pier Giorgio Frassati: Echi di memorie* (Genoa: Marietti, 1989), 170.

44. As Mussolini's government moved gradually from a traditional parliamentary party toward a dictatorship, Fascist violence against all political opposition, including the Catholic Popular Party, increased. So it took real courage for Pier Giorgio to openly wear this well-known symbol of the Catholic Party pinned to his lapel.

45. L. Frassati, *L'impegno sociale e politico*, 83.

46. Ibid., 77–80.

47. L. Frassati, *Pier Giorgio Frassati: I giorni*, 158–159.

48. Cf. B. Bongiovanni and F. Levi, *L'Università di Torino durante il fascismo* (Turin, 1976); M. C. Giuntella, "I circoli universitari cattolici nell'Italia settentrionale" in *Chiesa, Azione Cattolica e fascismo* (Milan: Vita e Pensiero, 1979).

49. The Italian Catholic University Federation, or FUCI, was an association of university students dedicated to being active in their community under the ideal of advancing the moral and cultural aspects of society. The organization viewed the time of university study as a fundamental period for the intellectual and civil growth of the person.

50. *Positio*, 5.

51. Ibid., vol. I, 283.

Chapter 5

52. G. A. Scaltriti, *Pier Giorgio Frassati e il suo Savonarola* (Milan: Edizioni Paoline, 1979).

53. P. G. Frassati, *Lettere*, 150.

54. In Pier Giorgio *Frassati, terziario domenicano: Ricordi, testimonianze, studi* (Bologna: Edizioni Studio Domenicano, 1991), 89.

55. L. Frassati, *Pier Giorgio Frassati: I giorni*, 77.

56. Dante, *Paradiso*, canto XXXIII, 371–372.

57. Ibid., 365.

58. P. G. Frassati, *Lettere*, 333.

59. Ibid., 260.

60. See M. Beltramo, "Il messaggio perenne di Pier Giorgio," in *Pier Giorgio Frassati a trent'anni dalla morte* (Turin, 1955), 29.

61. *Treatise on True Devotion to the Blessed Virgin Mary*, no. 35.

Chapter 6

62. Luciana Frassati, *Mio fratello Pier Giorgio: La fede* (Rome: Edizioni Paoline, 1954), 85.

63. Teresa of Jesus, *Esclamazioni*, 17, 4, in *Opere* (Rome: OCD, 1985).

64. L. Frassati, *La fede*, 182.

65. P. G. Frassati, *Lettere*, 280.

66. Dan Montgomery, *Essere se stessi* (Milan: Edizioni Paoline, 1998), 37.

67. Ibid., 36.

68. Luciana Frassati, *Il cammino di Pier Giorgio* (Milan: Rizzoli Editore, 1990), 180.

69. John Paul II, *Christifideles laici* (Boston: Pauline Books & Media, 1988), no. 16.

70. P. G. Frassati, *Lettere*, 179.

Chapter 7

71. Probably a reference to the House of Divine Providence founded by Saint Joseph Benedict Cottolengo as a home for the elderly, the physically and mentally handicapped, and for the poor and the sick.

72. Cf. *Positio*, vol. I, 297.

73. F. Antonioli, et al., *Pier Giorgio Frassati*, 52–53.

74. C. Casalegno, *Pier Giorgio Frassati*, 388.

75. C. Pera, "Un'uomo del XX secolo," in *Pier Giorgio Frassati, terziario domenicano*, 68–69.

76. L. Frassati, *Pier Giorgio Frassati: I giorni*, 170.

77. Luciana Frassati, *Mio fratello Pier Giorgio: La carita* (Rome: Edizione Paoline, 1951), 5.

78. I. A. Chiusano, "Santo con coraggio e allegria," in *La Voce del Popolo*, May 13, 1990.

79. P. G. Frassati, *Lettere*, 104–105.

Chapter 8

80. L. Frassati, *Pier Giorgio Frassati: I giorni*, 133–136.

81. R. Claude, S.J., *Attualità di Pier Giorgio Frassati* (Turin: SEI, 1960), 93.

82. P. G. Frassati, *Lettere*, 182.

83. L. Frassati, *Pier Giorgio Frassati: I giorni*, 160.

84. P. G. Frassati, *Lettere*, 330.

85. Cf. *Dossier: Hidalgo*.

86. P. G. Frassati, *Lettere*, 321–322.

87. L. Frassati, *La fede*, 91.

Chapter 9

88. L. Frassati, *Pier Giorgio Frassati: I giorni*, 137–138.

89. Ibid., 190.

90. Ibid., 313.

91. Ibid., 297.

92. Ibid., 253.

93. Ibid., 314.

94. F. Antonioli, et al., *Pier Giorgio Frassati*, 102.

95. P. G. Frassati, *Lettere*, 295.

96. L. Frassati, *Pier Giorgio Frassati: I giorni*, 155–156.

97. P. G. Frassati, *Lettere*, 289.

98. L. Frassati, *Pier Giorgio Frassati: I giorni*, 88.

99. Ibid., 36.

100. P. G. Frassati, *Lettere*, 301–302.

Chapter 10

101. P. G. Frassati, *Lettere*, 285.

102. Ibid., 261–262.

103. Ibid., 286.

104. Luciana Frassati, *Calendario di una vita: 1901–1925: Pier Giorgio Frassati* (Turin: Istituto La Salle, 1981).

105. Luciana Frassati, *Una vita mai spenta: Ultimi sei giorni di Pier Giorgio* (Turin: Editrice La Stampa), 95.

106. Ibid., 59.

107. C. Casalegno, *Pier Giorgio Frassati*, 376.

108. Luciana Frassati, *Mio fratello Pier Giorgio: La carità* (Rome: Edizioni Paoline, 1951), 171.

109. P. G. Frassati, *Lettere*, 174.

110. Luciana Frassati, *Mio fratello Pier Giorgio: La morte* (Reggio Emilia: Città Armoniosa, 1981), 97.

111. L. Frassati, *Pier Giorgio Frassati: I giorni*, 133–136.

112. L. Frassati, *Una vita mai spenta*, 115.

113. L. Ambrosini, "La leggenda pia già fiorisce," in *La Stampa*, July 7, 1925.

114. F. Turati, "Era veramente un uomo," in *La Giustizia*, July 8, 1925.

115. F. Antonioli, et al., *Pier Giorgio Frassati*, 25.

Chapter 11

116. John Paul II, "Homily for the Beatification of Pier Giorgio Frassati," *L'Osservatore Romano*, May 21–22, 1990.

117. John Paul II, discourse in Pollone, Italy, *L'Osservatore Romano*, July 17–18, 1989.

118. L. Frassati, *Man of the Beatitudes*, from introduction by Karl Rhaner (Slough, England: Saint Paul Publications, 1990), 8, 9.

119. P. G. Frassati, Lettere, 190.

Appendix C

120. Italian Episcopal Conference, *Catechism of Adults*, cf. La Verità vi farà liberi, 1995, no. 1089.

About the Author

Maria Di Lorenzo, a graduate in Modern Languages and a journalist, has worked for the daily newspaper, Il Tempo, for RAI, and for Vatican Radio. An expert in spirituality and religious issues, she is a regular contributor to various Catholic publications, an editor of Web sites dedicated to saints and exemplary people of our day, and author of several books.

Thank You.

Your purchase of this book and engagement with our other projects supports us in the work we do as Daughters of St. Paul. This book is the fruit of our consecrated life, prayer, and mission of communicating God's love.

We hold you and all your intentions in our prayers. We invite you to connect with us or send us prayer intentions at pauline.org.

Pauline
BOOKS & MEDIA